INSIGHT TO IMPACT

INSIGHT TO IMPACT

Empowering a New Generation of
Finance Leaders

STEPHANIE S. HOCKMAN

CERTIFIED

(H)

WRITTEN
BY HUMAN

ACKNOWLEDGMENTS

To my mom, who is my inspiration. I miss you every day.

To my dad, who taught me to speak my mind and how to be a good coach.

To Jim, my second dad, who taught me to be unapologetically successful and how to consider the strengths and weaknesses of others to help them develop and succeed.

To my brothers, who taught me to be tough.

To my grandmothers, who taught me the meaning of family and unconditional love.

To Chris, who taught me how to love.

To my kids, who have taught me patience, and a few new words, memes, and emojis.

To my friends, who have stood by me through laughter and tears, blunders, and successes.

To my mentors and colleagues, who taught me how to value my contribution to an organization.

To those who I do not consider friends, thank you for your poor actions. Your examples taught me what not to do and how not to treat others.

CONTENTS

Acknowledgments.. 5

Introduction 9

1. The Talent Equation 15
2. Insight Into The Process.. 25
3. The Alvista Loop Empowerment Process 37
4. Know Thyself.. 43
5. Reinforce Your Mindset 57
6. Lights, Camera, Action.. 67
7. Make It a Habit 73
8. Empower Yourself to Empower Others 81
9. Attracting Early-Career Talent.. 89
10. Navigating a Multigenerational Workforce..................... 95
11. Empowering Women to Empower Your Organization................103
12. Empowering an Industry..111

Conclusion... 115
Final Thought... 119
About the Author 127

INTRODUCTION

"Never underestimate the power you have to take your life in a new direction."

– Germany Kent

When it comes to talent, the finance industry likes to think it attracts the best. Money definitely talks, but what gets attention isn't what keeps attention. The industry has a stunningly high attrition rate of 18.6%, and retention trend analysis reveals that early-career talent — and especially diverse early-career talent — are staying in their roles for shorter and shorter periods before leaving for more welcoming environments.[1]

The result? A talent crisis, and not an easy one to address. I won't sugarcoat things for you. It will take serious action from within and support from without to fully remedy today's recruitment, retention, and development challenges.

---

[1]   Ufer, Tim. "The Millennial Turnover Problem in the Financial Services Industry [UPDATED 2024]." Hppy, 1 Dec. 2017, gethppy.com/employee-turnover/the-millennial-turnover-problem-in-the-financial-services-industry.

A Talent Shortage in a World of Abundance

The world's best and brightest regard the finance industry as one where it's difficult to get in, difficult to get ahead, and difficult to survive. There's also a persistent belief that to thrive in the space, you need to look a certain way and act a certain way (think Patagonia vests, formal, monochromatic, and male.)

For a time, it didn't matter to firms how they were perceived by entry-level and early-career talent. If you didn't like it, you could leave. If you didn't fit into the traditional mold, find the door. Who cared? There would always be more applicants in the pipeline, right?

Not anymore! These days, financial firms are realizing that their pipelines are waning, and it only gets worse as you move up the organizational hierarchy. High attrition rates, especially for women and traditionally underrepresented groups, mean a distinct lack of diversity in the middle and upper levels of most financial firms. As a result, the industry as a whole is aging out and falling behind on key aspects of competitiveness, resiliency, and innovation as the best and brightest make their careers elsewhere.

To reverse this course — to refill the pipelines and retain key early-career talent for later development into the leaders of the future — firms need to shift their approach to talent acquisition and development.

The Way Forward

Throughout this book, you will have the chance to see an approach that's working to nurture and develop the finance leaders of the future. It is distinctly different from what most institutions are currently doing and uniquely appealing to Millennial and Gen Z talent.

These groups, after all, represent what will soon be the largest age cohorts in the working world. Boomers are retiring, with the oldest members of Gen X right behind them. If the average Millennial hire in finance leaves their position after just 17 months, who will be around to replace your workforce, much less empower and drive it forward?

Making the choice to do talent differently means you can avoid being a company that becomes irrelevant. You will have the chance to not just attract but also retain and grow fresh talent to diversify and uplift your teams and your organization.

The Winning Combination: Attract, Grow, and Retain

The companies that are winning in today's talent environment have taken steps to make themselves an appealing place to work — not just at first glance but long-term and across multiple life and career stages. This is because it's not just about attracting applicants. Top companies understand that they need to demonstrate to top talent that their organization is worthy of a long-term commitment.

After all, working with thousands of collegiate, early-, and mid-career employees, I have seen firsthand that Millennials and Gen Zers aren't commitment-phobic. They simply prefer to work at firms where they feel seen and valued and where they have proof of their organization's investment in a mutually profitable, life-enhancing future. In those environments, their loyalty, drive, and performance are unparalleled, and they take pride in lifting their organizations to greater and greater heights.

Can you imagine your company filled with enthusiastic, engaged, and highly competent talent from the very foundations on up? Can you imagine keeping them in-house for years... maybe even decades... as they develop, grow, and thrive? Where instead of a self-fulfilling prophecy of turnover, you had a self-perpetuating cycle of achievement and improvement? What is out there that you *couldn't* achieve with a team like that behind you?

The Stakes Have Never Been Higher

The moment for taking action is now. Some 61% of financial professionals are 40+, and more than 25% of them lack any succession plan.[2] That's an incredible opportunity to promote fresh talent... if there was enough fresh talent being nurtured and developed within your organization.

Understanding what's happening — getting the real insights that make a difference — will help you shift and redesign your approach to talent in a way that appeals to the next generation

---

[2]   Reed, Jennifer Lea. "25% of Advisors near Retirement Lack a Succession Plan, Cerulli Says." Fa-Mag.com, FA Mag, 13 June 2022, www.fa-mag.com/news/1-in-4-advisors-nearing-retirement-lack-a-succession-plan-68291.html. Accessed 25 Nov. 2024.

of financial leaders. And, if you can attract, grow, and retain top talent, then your organization will thrive.

CHAPTER 1

The Talent Equation

"People are not your most important asset. The right people are."

– Jim Collins

Let's face it. The finance industry shapes the global economy. It moves money from those who have it to those who need it. Finance and the economy are interrelated and inform each other. So, why is the finance industry not more representative of a global economy and global society? The finance industry needs people to work in it, mold it, and move it, but more importantly, it needs the right people.

The most recent data available tells us there are about 136,000 finance professionals employed in the United States. Some 74% are men and 26% are women; women still earn just 85% of men's compensation. Ethnically, 72% are white, 10% are Hispanic or Latino, 6% are Black or African American, 8% are Asian, and 4% are other. Some 5% are part of the LGBTQ+ community.[3]

---

3   "Finance Professional Demographics and Statistics [2021]: Number of Finance Professionals in the US." Www.zippia.com, 29 Jan. 2021, www.zippia.com/finance-professional-jobs/demographics/

To equalize the talent equation, it's paramount that the finance industry shift its goal of attracting diverse talent. It must also retain and grow that diverse talent. I've seen firsthand how the industry has tried to navigate the diversity landscape but continues to struggle to truly create an industry representative of the composition of the global economy.

Unrealized Potential

Believe it or not, the problem is rather simple.

Lack of representation.

Representation isn't just about gender or race. True representation is attracting, growing, and retaining those with different experiences, backgrounds, and views. By creating an industry that is representative of the global economy and resembles the composition of the clients it represents, the more successful, profitable, and enduring the companies will be. Yet, this lack of diversity and representation is one of the main reasons companies have trouble finding and retaining top talent.

Potential employees don't see people who resemble them or share their experiences in these firms, so they hesitate to join. This becomes a self-fulfilling prophecy and reduces diversity within the organization, creating roadblocks to recruiting and retaining top talent. Less diversity decreases creativity and profitability. Ultimately, this holds companies back from realizing their full potential.

At this point, it becomes a business strategy problem. Finance firms are realizing that they leave value on the table when they fail to build and retain more diverse teams. The conversation is shifting from, "Why don't we have more diversity?" to, "What are we missing without it?" Diverse voices present new ideas and opportunities for growth. The talent is out there. But now, the industry needs to create pathways to attract, grow, and retain that talent, thereby creating representation, changing the industry's landscape, and eliminating the self-fulfilling prophecy.

Dynamic Challenges

Just because companies realize the importance of finding diverse talent doesn't mean that they *can* find that talent. And if they can find diverse talent and hire them (e.g. many investment banks have entry-level analyst classes with a 1:1 men-to-women ratio), they aren't changing their internal programs fast enough to grow and retain the early career talent. To attract, grow, and retain top talent takes intentional effort and planning. Companies need to think outside the box and take risks on new ideas and initiatives if they want to create a continuous flow of diverse talent.

Attract

Attracting top talent in the finance industry has always been a challenge. While progress has been made in this area, there's still a long way to go. Even though men and women are graduating from college in roughly equal numbers, there are fewer women entering finance organizations. Over the last decade, companies have worked hard to expand their candidate pool by launching specialized programs aimed at women, people of color, and the

LGBTQ+ community. These efforts have certainly widened the talent pool and brought more diversity into the hiring process.

Yet, attracting talent is only the first step. Getting people in the door is great, but if the internal culture doesn't support their growth and success, if the organization doesn't have diverse representation throughout the company, it's all for nothing. Many firms struggle to keep their new hires engaged once they're on board. They have specialized programs and opportunities that cater to diverse populations, but they're not getting the outcomes they want. They might invite talent to the "party," but without the right environment, support, and representation these individuals often do not stay.

Grow

The challenge of growing talent ties directly into retention. If employees don't see clear development opportunities, they're not going to stick around. People, especially Millennials and Gen Zers, want structured development programs and mentorship. They seek to both grow professionally and to know that their firm cares about them and their career development.

This is where executive coaching can make a big difference. Although some firms provide executive coaching at senior levels, providing talent development and executive coaching at early- and mid-level stages of a career can be the differentiating factor — demonstrating that the company's culture is one of valuing employees at every level of their career progression. By providing a whole-person approach to professional development throughout the organization and at every level of the organization, firms can establish an explicit example of how they care about developing and retaining their talent. As talent feels invested in, they develop loyalty toward their company. As they grow in their roles, additional coaching can help these emerging leaders shift from doing the work to managing it effectively, paving the way for additional growth within their careers.

Companies that invest in their talent at every stage in their careers will not only retain their top talent but help them thrive in their roles. This creates loyalty and longevity which in turn creates representation throughout the firm.

Retain

Retaining talent, especially women and persons of color, is even harder than attracting. Women, in particular, often face life milestones — starting a family, taking care of elderly parents — that can pull them away from work. So the question becomes, how are companies responding to these changes? Unfortunately, many firms still haven't figured out how to adequately support women through times of transition. Most offer maternity leave, but there are more needs that have to be met. Return-to-work programs, flexible schedules, and ongoing support during major life changes can make or break a person's experience. Without these, women are left feeling like they have to choose between their personal lives and their careers. This is a vicious cycle. Women feel they have to leave the industry, and then representation disappears. It becomes more difficult for others to see a path of growth and success at the firm when they can't see themselves at the organization.

Another well-intentioned yet often unsuccessful strategy is the creation of affinity groups. While these groups are meant to foster a sense of inclusion, they can sometimes feel superficial or forced. Employees may sense that these efforts are more about optics than real, meaningful change, especially if initiatives that come out of affinity group discussions are never implemented. The problem is that companies think merely having the programs in place will solve their retention issues. However, when they don't genuinely engage with feedback or really think about outcomes, the program falls flat, and top talent may walk out the door.

Additional Complexities

While we've explored many of the challenges with attracting, growing, and retaining top talent, there are also additional complexities to consider for a realistic view of the landscape. The truth is that we have a new generation of professionals coming in, and the traditional ways of onboarding and training no longer work.

Today's Gen Z professionals are not like their predecessors, such as Gen Xers or Baby Boomers, who were trained in a very different environment. Financial services firms have not fully adapted their training methods to address the mindset and expectations of younger generations. Gen Z approaches their careers with distinct values — they crave flexibility, prioritize work-life alignment, and view their role in the workplace through a different lens. Yet, they often encounter antiquated, rigid systems and expectations that don't align with how they want to work and live. They are being asked to conform to historical cultures when they want to work where their authentic self is accepted.

This generational disconnect can often frustrate both sides. Employers may perceive Gen Z as disengaged or uninterested when, in reality, they're simply looking for a workplace that better suits their expectations. When organizations fail to adapt to those expectations, they risk alienating talent. When they alienate that talent, talent leaves — reducing diverse representation and, again, creating a self-fulfilling prophecy of no representation.

Going beyond generational shifts, the industry must also navigate the complexities of a multigenerational workforce. Each generation brings different expectations for communication, work styles, and professional boundaries. For example, Baby Boomers and Gen Xers expect formal communication, typically via email. On the other hand, Gen Z's inclination to text colleagues directly can be perceived as unprofessional. These expectations can lead to tension unless both sides learn to understand and respect each other's preferences.

Then there's the issue of gender dynamics. Women in finance face unique hurdles. The industry, still largely male-dominated, often overlooks the additional demands on women's time. While many male counterparts have stay-at-home partners, women in finance typically juggle professional responsibilities with personal ones without the same level of at-home support. So, women must continually prove themselves while managing more outside of work than their male colleagues.

Interestingly, this is not the only place creating tension for women. Women often feel pressured by other women in the industry. Those who choose not to have children or who eschew traditional family roles may believe they deserve to advance faster or earn more than their peers who are balancing family life. This internal friction creates a layer of complexity that isn't often acknowledged but significantly impacts the retention and growth of women in the finance industry.

All of these challenges — generational divides, gender dynamics, and a lack of diversity — combine to create a cycle that's hard to break. Companies that fail to recognize these shifts risk losing top talent to firms that are more adaptable. By understanding and addressing the needs of a multigenerational, diverse workforce, financial services firms can create an environment where all employees can thrive. They can create a cycle of attracting, growing, and retaining talent that results in representation. This, in turn, leads to greater creativity, innovation, and profitability.

Consider This

What would your organization look like if the top of the organizational chart was as diverse as the entry level? What would your organization's innovation and results be if you had more diverse talent at every level? What would it look like if the lack of representation faded away and you were able to cultivate a diverse talent pool where underrepresented groups could thrive? When organizations commit to diversifying themselves, they solve a significant part of the complex equation for attracting and holding onto talent. They realize the potential that resides in all of those diverse voices.

A workforce that mirrors the diversity of clients also leads to enhanced understanding and improved relationships. Employers are able to tap into the unique experiences and insights of their teams and become better equipped to respond to the needs of the market. This, in turn, allows firms to build stronger connections with clients who see themselves represented in the organizations with whom they choose to partner.

Be inspired. Be inspiring.

Finally, organizations that diversify their leadership create a culture of mentorship and inspiration. They create representation. A varied leadership team can share their experiences and lift others like them up as they climb. As more of these individuals ascend to leadership roles, they have more opportunities to mentor emerging talent. I like to say, "Be inspired. Be inspiring." This cyclical dynamic of being inspired by others to succeed and then inspiring others to do the same is one of the best ways to build potential within an organization.

Yet, this complex equation is also not so easily solved. The journey requires a lot of intentionality and sustained effort. However, with the right mindset and desire to implement non-traditional strategies, this change is possible. In the next two chapters, we'll delve into my background and how my experiences created the Alvista Loop Empowerment Process, a continuous loop of insight, understanding, action, and habits that unlock purpose, performance, and impact.

CHAPTER 2

Insight Into The Process

"It doesn't matter who you are, where you come from. The ability to triumph begins with you - always."

– Oprah Winfrey

We've talked briefly about the finance industry, but let me tell you my experience. A lifetime of lived experiences has fine-tuned my talent development and executive coaching skills, culminating in the Alvista Loop Empowerment Process. I thought about titling the book *Farm to Finance: Lessons Learned From Living Life Outside My Comfort Zone*. Instead, I decided on *Insight to Impact* to demonstrate how my life experiences, both failures and successes, can help generate a new generation of finance leaders.

Like everyone's, my life has been a series of decisions and experiences that have shaped who I am today. When I reflect on 50+ years of living — of which over 30 years have been in the finance industry — the one thing I know is that without failure and living outside my comfort zone, I could never be the person I am today. I use my experiences to actively listen, understand, and create a real empowerment process, a ripple effect that creates a finance industry more representative of society. I understand the complex world of finance and know what it feels like to forge a path in what's been a traditionally male-dominated landscape. Through my journey, I've learned that embracing change is a powerful catalyst for personal and professional growth. It's that philosophy that I bring to my talent development programs and executive coaching relationships.

Built From Experience

I grew up on a cattle farm in Oklahoma, where every decision impacted the family's livelihood. If my parents didn't sell the cattle at a good price, I wouldn't have new tennis shoes for school. As a result, I developed a strong work ethic and an early understanding of how cattle futures and, by extension, the economy played an integral role in my family's livelihood. I quickly learned that the more effort I put into my responsibilities, like feeding the cows, baling hay, or helping my grandfather birth calves, the better the outcomes for my family and myself. This foundational lesson shaped my understanding of success — it's rarely handed to you. You have to create success through work ethic, grit, and adaptability.

If you look at my life over the last 50+ years, it's been a series of changes where I had to gain insight to create an impact on my own life and that of others. There have been geographical shifts, from Oklahoma to Texas to Illinois to California to Montana to New York to Massachusetts; professional shifts going from the University of Texas at Austin to Arthur Andersen, Bank of America, BNP Paribas, and Amherst College; and personal shifts from being single to married to having kids. At each point, I constantly leaned into the need to face the fears that swelled up inside to create my own path forward.

My first experience outside my comfort zone came on a dare when I was 6 years old. I was at home on our farm with my brothers. They had a rope tied to a tree branch near our large pond. They were swinging from the rope into the pond. It was a hot day, and it looked so refreshing, even if it was the pond where the cattle would go to wade in the water.

I was really scared, but in typical 'big brother' fashion, they egged me on and teased me until I swallowed my fear — and my pride. I grabbed the rope, walked back about 5 steps, and ran forward to swing into the water. Unfortunately, I had not grabbed high enough on the rope and dragged my legs on the tree roots as I went, barely, into the pond. I was totally embarrassed and had a huge scrape on my leg that ended up being a scar. That became my first mark of bravery, as I like to call it. I had faced my fear.

The lesson learned was that even when things don't work out, you always learn something if you are open to seeing beyond the failure. The pond dare taught me that I needed to grab higher on the rope and that I should have asked my brothers the best way to swing into the pond or at least paid more attention to see what they did. I learned that sometimes it takes others to help you live outside your comfort zone and face your fears. I learned that even if I hadn't done something before, like swinging on a rope into a pond, it didn't mean I couldn't do it. I learned that failure was an option and one that taught me more than if I had succeeded. I took those lessons and tried to apply them throughout my life.

Another shift happened when I was twelve. My parents divorced. I went to live with my mom in Tulsa. I had to step outside my comfort zone to make new friends. I was not a confident social butterfly. I was incredibly self-conscious. I wasn't pretty or skinny. I was the epitome of a tomboy, and although I had been proud of that on the farm, moving to Tulsa — the 'big city' — I just didn't know how to fit in. I had to learn!

I pushed myself to make friends and find my place. I tried out for the 7th-grade basketball team, and even though I wasn't as good as so many of the other players and definitely not as tall, I knew that I loved playing, and that showed to the coaches. I made great friends playing ball and learned that my love for the game could be an example for other teammates even if they had more skill. I also didn't like speaking in public, but I decided to try out for the debate team. Although I think everyone else saw my skills to 'negotiate' and win arguments, I didn't know I had such abilities. Going into debate practice for the first time and learning how to craft arguments and make compelling statements was way outside my comfort zone and one of my biggest growth experiences. These are two examples of ways I learned to face my fears and step into the unknown; even during the awkward middle school years.

As high school graduation approached, having grown up in Oklahoma, I wanted to stretch beyond where most of my friends and classmates were going to college. When I chose the University of Texas, it was a bold move — one that took me far from the comfort of familiar faces and places. This turned into a time of immense growth. I learned to balance coursework with involvement in different organizations like Orange Jackets, my sorority (Alpha

Chi Omega), and the Business Council. I learned to appreciate the differences in the people that surrounded me. I loved my 5 years at UT, and I realized that I was increasingly comfortable with learning and experiencing new things by stepping out of my comfort zone. I found comfort in the uncomfortable.

This knowledge, that real success came from embracing the unknown and not fearing the unfamiliar, led me to take another jump upon graduation. I decided not to stay in OK or TX, and instead moved to Chicago to take a tax consultant role at Arthur Andersen. It was also a city so different from anywhere else I had lived. My world expanded, and so did I. I made new friends and great professional connections, branched out to even be a volunteer coach of an 8th-grade girls' basketball team, and established the first junior board of the Off the Street Club. My prior life experiences to that point emboldened me to take chances and continue to thrive in the uncomfortable zone of new experiences.

The great thing about moving to a new city and starting with a 'blank slate' is that it gives you the opportunity to really reinvent yourself and go after something you might otherwise never pursue. It's also a factor of being in your 20s when you feel that anything is possible and you are invincible. Obviously not true, but at the time, living in a new place, making new friends, and learning new things at work and in volunteer activities shaped so many of my core values, especially the importance of building relationships and paying it forward.

Probably one of the hardest lessons about living outside my comfort zone came during this early phase of my professional life.

As I started my career at Arthur Andersen, I was fortunate enough to find a group of individuals and, especially, two mentors who ignited my passion for the financial services industry. Although my work as a tax consultant was helping hedge funds, investment partnerships, and family offices use strategies that were within the tax law, it provided an opportunity to be creative and find ways to help our clients be more profitable. I was good at my job, and the logic of the tax law seemed natural to me. I quickly progressed in my career, creating impactful solutions to complex issues. I gained a reputation for "getting it done" with my colleagues and clients. I also took on additional responsibilities including recruiting young talent and training them at the Arthur Andersen facility in St. Charles, Illinois.

Unfortunately, I didn't *love* my job. I was good at it and could have become a partner, but I didn't love it. I found that after I had gained proficiency in my abilities to provide solutions to clients, I became complacent. I got bored, a theme throughout my professional career. So, to liven things up, I took the initiative to grow by trying to create a new group dedicated to the growth of the hedge fund practice. I didn't ask permission but instead started creating a business plan on how we could grow our clients and services provided. I worked extra hours to create a database of prospects and ways that we could market our group to a broader audience. When that group wasn't able to be formed (bureaucracy and politics were hard lessons to learn) I took time to reflect on what I really wanted.

During a work trip to the Cayman Islands, I decided to take a few vacation days and relax on the beach. I wanted to take time to reflect on what I wanted in life and reflect on my time at Arthur

Andersen. I had poured my heart and soul into building a hedge fund advisory practice, only to feel overlooked by ten of the eleven male partners in the group. As I sat on the beach contemplating the safety of the known versus what made me happy, I watched the sunrise with a new vision for my future. I faced the comfort of the known: the partnership track, my ability to be a great tax consultant, and the team of mentors and colleagues focused on developing me and others. I asked myself if that was enough, or did I want more?

After much soul-searching, I made the tough decision to leave the firm without another job lined up. I stepped away from comfort to embrace the unknown. It was terrifying, but I had learned that sometimes stepping back and reassessing your path is a crucial part of growth. In those moments of uncertainty, I confronted the fear of the unknown head-on. I trusted myself to know that it would work out because I would work hard enough to make it so.

One of the hardest moments in my professional career came when I returned from the Cayman Islands and walked into my mentor's office, the one partner who I felt understood me and my goals. I told him I was resigning. It was difficult because he was not only a mentor but also a friend. Relationships are everything to me, and I was determined to handle the resignation in the best way possible to preserve our friendship and his mentorship. As we've remained friends, I know the conversation and the situation were a success as well as a growth experience. These sorts of candid conversations and ways to be true to yourself and honest with others are hallmark characteristics of who I am. It's also the approach I like to take with my clients.

That step away from tax consulting started me on a different growth trajectory in the financial services industry. Taking a leap into the unknown world of banking and prime services led to 15 years of continuous professional growth and the opportunity to build global teams and create programs that focused on talent development and mentorship. Although embedded in large organizations, I found ways to be innovative and be an entrepreneur. To realign resources, people, and teams to create more efficient procedures with the goal of developing people, helping them grow, and focusing on clients. It was my opportunity to follow my path and create what I knew to be a better way.

I also realized that I didn't have to be 100% qualified for a job to 'go for it.' It was knowing from prior experience that just because I hadn't done it didn't mean I couldn't do it. I knew that by seizing the opportunity, I could fail, or I could succeed. It was about being able to step outside my comfort zone that allowed me those experiences to grow. Similar to what Sheryl Sandberg said in her book *Lean In*, you have to take that seat at the table and be ready to speak up and seize the opportunity. You also have to be willing to treat your career — and your life — as a jungle gym, not necessarily a ladder. The ability to move laterally or in a different direction allowed me to truly grow.

A good example was when I was at Bank of America. I was in the Chicago office and doing really well working with clients and making sure we were providing the best service while maximizing the client's revenue potential. We implemented several of my ideas, including publishing the *Starting a Hedge Fund* guide and creating a client analysis of operational resources to revenue ratio to make sure we were pricing each client in a way that was beneficial for the client and the bank. I was really happy with how things were going with my clients, in the office, and my life in Chicago. It was during that comfortable phase when a Managing Director at Bank of America approached me about moving to San Francisco. Although I had to check with my husband about moving (we had been married less than 3 months and he was working for the U.S. Navy in Bahrain), I took the opportunity to move us to a new city and help revamp the San Francisco office. By taking advantage of the opportunity, I experienced a new city, a new set of clients — and their problems — and found new ways to grow professionally. It was also a time and place where my personal life was changing (married, 2 kids), and a major career shift to BNP Paribas that led to the next 7 years of growth. If I hadn't taken the opportunity to 'start over' in a new office, with new colleagues, and in a new town with new situations, I would likely have become bored in Chicago and started searching for that next opportunity.

These examples go on and on throughout my life. The ability to face my fears and step outside my comfort zone could lead to accomplishments or failures, but most importantly, it taught me that each experience holds a lesson. Even better? I learned how to constantly feel uncomfortable, which results in the most growth and the best that life has to offer. I learned to be proactive and assertive. I learned that the anxiety I felt was energy and fuel to push me forward. I learned that as I approach each situation, each task, and each opportunity, I can learn, pivot, adjust, and grow.

These lessons became even more poignant in 2015 when I faced one of the toughest challenges of my career — being fired from my role as a Managing Director at BNP Paribas. The experience was a harsh wake-up call, a reminder of how swiftly the tide can turn in this industry and the importance of learning who to trust. As I mentioned above, relationships matter. However, not all relationships are like the one I had with my Arthur Andersen mentor — supportive, growth-minded, and positive. At BNP Paribas, I found out the hard way that, at times in the finance industry, those that you trusted and felt were mentors, allies, or supporters, when faced with making the right, ethical decision, would choose their self-preservation. This experience taught me a lot about trusting the right people and knowing that there is no one better to trust than yourself — a theme that is often the topic of exploration with my executive coaching clients. In this situation, instead of succumbing to despair, I chose to view it as an opportunity. I began to see how being fired — while painful — could also be a doorway to new beginnings.

In the face of adversity, I became determined to turn my struggles into something meaningful. This mindset became a cornerstone of my work with emerging talent in finance. I transitioned from investment banking to a role focused on developing a program at Amherst College. There, I had the privilege of mentoring young minds, particularly Gen Zers and Millennials, and guiding them through exploring the finance industry to define their path.

Empowerment begins with acknowledging the unique challenges we face and sharing our experiences to foster a culture of inclusivity. As we explore the Alvista Loop Empowerment Process, remember that your experiences — both the triumphs and the setbacks — are building blocks for your future. Each moment of uncertainty is an opportunity for growth, every decision a chance to define your narrative, and every step an ability to blaze your own trail.

In this book, we will delve deeper into the practical strategies and insights that have emerged from my experiences to create my talent development and executive coaching process. Together, we'll explore how to empower not just ourselves but every generation of finance leaders.

CHAPTER 3

The Alvista Loop Empowerment Process

"Deconstruction creates knowledge. Reconstruction creates value."

– James Clear

My life experiences are the foundation for the Alvista Loop Empowerment Process. It is a framework, but the truth is that professional development isn't a one-size-fits-all journey. It's unique to everyone and shaped by diverse backgrounds, aspirations, and challenges. The empowerment process is about creating a tailored series of steps designed to enable individuals to gain insight, power, control, and confidence over decisions made. It helps foster self-awareness, develop skills, promote the ability to influence others and organizations, and maximize performance. It is a continuous loop of growth that takes one's insights and generates impact.

Throughout this book, I'll share parts of my life and show how the Alvista Loop Empowerment Process can help improve your understanding of yourself and your organization. We'll explore topics on how to embrace your unique identity and appreciate the perspectives and experiences of others. We'll talk about how reflection can help you discover your ideal career and, ultimately, an organization that aligns with your values and goals.

We'll also look at the importance of blazing your own trail and breaking out of the norm. Finding and retaining diverse talent requires a shift from traditional, monochromatic viewpoints to ones of possibility and adaptability.

Fostering a culture of inclusion goes hand in hand with that and is a key value for this process. Employers seeking to attract, grow, and retain top talent must create spaces that appreciate and help other members appreciate differences.

At the end of the day, when employees feel empowered, they are more engaged and productive. More importantly, they are likely to stay and empower others to do the same.

Empowering the Company

Many organizations hesitate to invest in this type of employee development because of cost concerns. They want to know that what they're putting in is actually going to affect that bottom line.

Rather than seeing these investments as mere expenses, I encourage leaders to ask themselves what this future is truly worth. What does it mean for a company to attract diverse talent? How does fostering an inclusive culture translate into improved employee retention and satisfaction? How can empowerment create a positive cycle of growth in the workforce?

One firm I've worked with truly believes in executive coaching, especially for those on the rise to the partner level. What's fantastic about this organization is that while the founder is male, the Number 2 person and many on the management committee are female.

As the company grew, they noticed it still felt very male-dominated. To address this, they not only established a women's affinity group but also focused on diversity hiring to expand their pool of female candidates. By attracting more women, they've created opportunities for those individuals. They bring in executive coaches like me, who work with their talent to develop their presence and advance in their careers. They understand the value of providing resources that help their employees grow their skills and their ability to lead — creating the next generation of finance leaders.

This approach has led to a self-fulfilling prophecy where **empowered women help other women succeed.** They've realized that having someone like me — who has experience as a woman who reached the Managing Director level — can help them see that it's possible to balance motherhood and a successful career. I provide insights into the nuts and bolts of achieving that balance, offering a third-party resource for confidential conversations.

Another great example is a firm I know that truly embraces not just attracting but also growing and retaining its diverse talent. This investment firm created an 18-month rotational program focused on bringing non-traditional students into the organization. The new hires spend 18 months learning about aspects of the business and completing a capstone project focused on matching their interests with ways to improve and grow the firm. At the end of 18 months, these "not so new hires" are placed in a part of the organization that combines their interests with where they can have the most impact.

I remember working with one of the first participants in this program. When asked why he stayed at the firm for over 5 years, especially as his classmates and friends were on their second or third finance firms, he stated, "Why would I leave a place that knows me, my dreams, my aspirations, and seeks to utilize those in ways that are best for me and the organization?"

This firm is a great example of how listening and understanding their colleagues, allowing them to be themselves, and finding places of value in the organization creates a feeling of loyalty and belonging. A family that they call home.

These are two examples of the Alvista Loop Empowerment Process, which aligns individual growth with organizational objectives. The reality is when you empower people, you empower your company.

Empowering the Individual

To empower the company, you have to empower the individual. I have a lot of experience working with individuals of diverse backgrounds who want to better understand themselves and grow their skills to become even more valuable to their organizations while being true to themselves.

When it comes to individuals, the primary outcome of the Alvista Loop Empowerment Process is simple: it helps you achieve your professional and personal milestones. The idea is to discover the goals you want for yourself and to reach them. Easy, right?

The trick is that so many of us don't know what we want, and even if we do, we don't know how to get there. That's where this process excels.

A great example I often use as insight with my clients happened during the summer of 2008, leading up to the financial crisis. At that time, I was living in Texas at my parents' house; yes, I was 37 years old with 2 small kids, and I had moved back in so my mom could help me with the kids while my husband went to Kentucky to be with his dying mother. It was a hard decision to move to Dallas when Bank of America was in a bake-off to sell the prime services division and potentially stunt my career progression. However, I worked twice as hard to be an integral part of the transition team. It was when the sale was over that I had to make another tough decision.

I had been thinking that it was time to "retire" and move the family to Montana where we wanted to raise the kids. Then, BNP Paribas made me an offer I couldn't refuse. They allowed me to move to Montana, have an apartment in NYC, and continue to build out global relationship management teams in the U.S., London, and Hong Kong all while working from home every other week. I like to think I was a WFH mom before it became popular during the pandemic. Thanks to BNP Paribas empowering me to further develop my professional career while having the personal life I wanted, I was empowered to help grow the women's initiatives for the company. I often recommend a similar approach to my clients, helping them empower their talent to empower the overall organization.

Built by People

These are the kinds of issues companies tend to overlook, and they're also the reason that organizations struggle to retain talent. If your workers are underpaid, overworked, and don't see themselves achieving what they want out of life, they're going to leave. But, if you can pivot to help your talent achieve their goals within your organization, they become happier, satisfied, and more productive.

Companies are built by people. When you invest in people, you strengthen your foundation and workforce. Yet, individuals also have a responsibility. It is challenging for organizations to meet individual needs if individuals don't know what they want or have the courage to advocate for it. In the next four chapters, we'll explore the focal points of the Alvista Loop Empowerment Process. We'll begin with how it helps people better understand themselves and what they want and need.

CHAPTER 4

Know Thyself

"Be yourself, everyone else is already taken."

– Oscar Wilde

When my kids were little and misbehaved, their dad and I would give them a time-out. We wanted them to sit and think about what they had done, hoping they'd learn from it. That wasn't how I was raised. Growing up in Oklahoma in the 1970s, my parents had what they called the "Board of Education," and it had its own hard way of correcting me and my brothers when we acted up.

Things were very different when I became a parent in 2006 and 2007. Talk about being outside my comfort zone! There's no manual on how to raise kids. Sure, there are plenty of books, but every parent and every child is different. Parenting, for me, felt like drinking from a firehose. I often felt like I was drowning in failure — unsure why my kids did certain things, why they cried, or how to fix it. I quickly realized that sometimes I needed to give *myself* a time-out. I had to step away, reflect, and get my emotions in check so I could approach things rationally.

I've found the same to be true in business.

The key to making meaningful changes and feeling professionally and personally successful is understanding who you are now, who you want to become, and what changes you need to undergo to bridge that gap. Knowing yourself requires taking a time-out — time to step back and reflect on the fact that you are a product of all your experiences. These experiences are a critical part of who you are and why you do what you do. Creating the space to know yourself helps you ultimately unlock your purpose, impact, and performance. This is the start of the Alvista Loop Empowerment Process. We actively listen and ask questions to help our clients reflect on who they are and the goals they want to achieve.

The Importance of Knowing Yourself

You may feel like this phase of the process is primarily for individuals. But if you're an employer who wants to attract, retain, and grow quality talent, you'll first need to understand who and what talent sees when they walk in your door. That requires insight, which requires knowing yourself, knowing your talent, and knowing how your company is perceived. What is your company culture? How is that reflected in your people? Do your people embody your company values?

I've found that most people, particularly business leaders, don't take the time to stop and truly reflect both on themselves and their organization. Who are they, really? Who do they want to become in their personal and professional lives? Too often, the persona we bring to the office differs from the one we have at home. But what persona do we want to create to be truly successful?

You have to know yourself, yes — but you also need to be authentic. You can't bring a version of yourself to the office that's disconnected from who you truly are. Authenticity is essential for real success. Talent — people — are drawn to authenticity. People want to know the people they are working for and with are exactly who they say they are, and they want to have permission to be the same.

Be true to yourself. Be authentic. Be present.

After becoming a parent, I learned a crucial "trick of the trade" — the power of taking a time-out. It was a game-changer. Giving myself even a few minutes, or sometimes hours, to sit quietly and reflect helped me make more rational decisions. It gave me the space to think about what really mattered and how I wanted to move forward. It allowed me to step back, see the bigger picture, and figure out what I wanted and how to get there.

If you want to make effective change, this step in the process is critical. Diving into self-reflection helps you gain clarity on who you are, where you want to go, and what changes you need to bridge the gap. Make no mistake. This will require courage. You may not always like what you see. One of my favorite mantras is to be true to yourself, be authentic, and be present. The results are worth it. Or for the Swifties, live by Taylor Swift's motto, "If they don't like you for being yourself, be yourself more."

One example of when I was true to myself was in 2006. I was living in San Francisco, running the West Coast relationship management team at Bank of America. This was during a lot of transitions happening at the firm that created challenges for me to continue maximizing revenue from our clients. To give you a little insight, one meeting I had with a long-standing client was the third meeting in as many months with that client where I had to deliver disappointing news about services we were no longer going to provide. It was a meeting similar to hundreds of other meetings I had to do. It was a difficult time in the industry as I was challenged to continue increasing revenue from clients when we were decreasing service offerings. I could have sugar-coated things, but that's not my style. I was forthright and candid with my client. I chose to be my authentic self. In return, the client appreciated the approach, and we moved forward with a mutually beneficial relationship.

It was at this time in my career that another client offered me a job to become COO of his hedge fund. It was flattering that he thought of me and my skills. At the time, I was eight months pregnant with my son. It would have been the easy route to take the new job, have a few months of maternity leave, and then start the new COO position, leaving the challenging circumstances at Bank of America behind. However, I took the time to think about what I wanted at that point in my career. Where did I feel I could add the most value? Where could I have the biggest impact? I had always viewed my career purpose to be building relationships and being the most impactful member of my firm. I ultimately decided to stay at Bank of America, which set me on a path to running global teams and expanding the influence and impact I had not only on our clients but also internally with our early-career professionals. It was a perfect example of where I could have pivoted but that would not have been true to who I knew myself to be, another lesson I often incorporate into my executive coaching sessions.

What You Should Get Out of This

There is a lot of content out there about self-reflection and the importance of authenticity. They'll take you in various directions, depending on their focus. For our purpose, reflection is all about gaining clarity on your goals.

You may find, after a period of reflection, that you don't have to change, or at least not in a dramatic fashion. You can know yourself and be perfectly happy with who you are. In this case, it's more about asking, "How do I improve from here?" Or, as Marshall Goldsmith points out in his book *What Got You Here Won't Get You There*, even successful people need to recognize ways that they can improve to get to that next level. So, the process becomes more about getting clear on what the next step looks like. That's still not an easy task.

For me, a great example of when I was happy with who I was but still feeling held back was in October 2000. As you'll recall, I had been working at Arthur Andersen for about six and a half years. I was fortunate to join a great company and work with amazing people. At the time, I was focused on creating a new group at Arthur Andersen aimed at the global growth of the hedge fund practice, just as hedge funds were becoming the "go-to" investment vehicle.

What I didn't realize then was the amount of office politics and bureaucracy that comes with working in a large global organization like Arthur Andersen. I knew I could help grow an incredible practice, but I didn't have the experience or political capital to make it happen, which became frustrating.

It was then, after sitting on that Cayman Island beach, that I realized my true value was not in dealing with the bureaucracy and ten of eleven partners who didn't value me. My value was in creating and enhancing people and processes. So, I resigned. After that, I took a time-out and reflected. I took three months to consider my next move. I loved hedge funds and the investment industry, but being a tax consultant wasn't challenging enough for me. I decided to become a 'recovering accountant' and start the next chapter in my professional career — providing financing and services to hedge funds at Bank of America's prime brokerage division. That decision set me on a successful 15-year career path.

Your reflections may not lead to as dramatic a change as mine did. Perhaps they'll reveal that your organization needs a shift in policy. Maybe you'll discover that you are seeking jobs that you aren't really interested in. Whatever your reflection reveals, don't ignore it. That's part of who you are and a crucial part of knowing and assessing yourself.

Assessing Yourself

Not everyone can spend reflection days on a beach, and not everyone has the financial means to explore their options for 3 months. Even if they can, they may not be able to understand their thoughts, feelings, and values in a way that helps them take actionable steps toward change. External assessments can be a powerful tool for learning about yourself and how other people perceive you, as well as give you clarity on changes you can make to better connect with people. There are a variety of assessments available, depending on your needs, including the

MBTI personality test, 360-degree feedback, the DiSC personality test, and the Hogan assessment.

The Hogan Assessment

At Alvista Loop, we love using the Hogan assessment. This is a favorite among many finance professionals. It breaks down personality traits into two categories: your "sunny side" and your "dark side."

The sunny side shows how you typically operate when everything is going well. It highlights your strengths, skills, and the qualities that make you an effective team member. Conversely, the dark side reveals how you respond under stress, providing valuable insights into the challenges you might face.

What we often find is that the person we are when things are calm isn't necessarily who we are under pressure. The goal is to make adjustments and foster growth by adjusting behaviors in those stressful moments.

We use assessments to give us a baseline. We'll go through them and understand how the person is perceived by others and how they perceive themselves. If there's no existing assessment, we might need to conduct a Hogan or MBTI assessment from scratch. No matter the assessment, the key takeaway is always about how clients see themselves versus how others — like direct reports, bosses, or clients — see them.

The insights result in actionable change. Understanding yourself fosters authenticity, but that understanding and authenticity should be wielded tactically. Your insights should result in actionable change. If your assessment reveals that your personality is quieter and less assertive, you may find that aligns with your experiences of getting looked over and ignored. That doesn't always mean you need to get loud and aggressive, especially if that's not your authentic self. You may find different ways to assert yourself and your opinion so that people pay attention, if that's your goal.

The key here is to take time to reflect, know yourself and your goals, and to balance staying true to who you are while also positioning yourself for success as you define it.

Expanding My Own Perspective

When I was at BNP Paribas, I was working hard to get promoted to Managing Director, but I got overlooked in my first year of consideration. When I asked my boss why I wasn't promoted, he simply said, "I didn't know you wanted to be Managing Director." It was like a splash of cold water in my face. I realized I had never verbalized what I wanted — the promotion. During the next year, I made it clear what I wanted. We went through our annual 360 assessment process, and I really started to pay attention to how others perceived me in a professional capacity. I made it obvious, both in my words and my actions, that I was ready to be Managing Director.

One key takeaway from the assessment process was that I always saw myself as forthright and candid. My clients, like the one in San Francisco, saw me as honest. However, many of my colleagues — especially the men — viewed me as a bull in a china shop. When I was going after something, they saw me as someone who would steamroll over everyone else. Now, I could have argued that it was their own (male) insecurity, but instead, I used my self-assessment and the 360-degree feedback to gain valuable insight into other people's perspectives and began to tailor my actions accordingly while still being my authentic self.

It wasn't about changing who I was; it was about adjusting how I allowed others to perceive me. I realized that while I didn't want to be less forthright, I needed to consider how my delivery might come across. The assessment helped me recognize that in certain situations, my candidness was perceived as aggressive. So, I focused on changing my verbal and nonverbal communication to make it easier for my colleagues, especially the men in the organization, to hear what I had to say without feeling threatened by that "bull in the china shop."

For example, I was advocating to revitalize our summer analyst program at BNP Paribas. I was facing a lot of resistance at the cost of the internship. This was a project I was passionate about. I wanted to develop the next generation of leaders at the firm and our current internship program was not getting the right talent in the door. Instead of being as impassioned as I would originally have been, I made my case for revamping the internship more quantitative and demonstrated the mid- and long-term benefits of getting the right interns and having them add value for their 10 weeks at the firm so they would want to return full-time. I also chose to sit at the conference room table with my colleagues to give my presentation rather than standing in front of them "lecturing." This approach resonated with my audience and helped us secure the revising of the summer analyst program, demonstrating another way I could add value by empowering others and paving the way for my promotion to Managing Director the following year.

Be Younique

In Ayn Rand's *Atlas Shrugged*, John Galt, an inventor and philosopher, embodies the belief in the power of the human mind and the right of individuals to use their minds for themselves. He stands in stark contrast to the collective social and economic structure that embraces mediocrity. I've re-read the book at least three times since my first exposure to it in college, each time discovering more about myself and how individual contributions create diversity, innovation, and inclusion. I may not be Dagny Taggart, the protagonist of *Atlas Shrugged*, but I know my individuality makes me valuable.

Do *you* understand your value?

The workplace often pushes toward conformity, encouraging a herd mentality where blending in feels like the safest choice. However, this approach stifles creativity and hinders professional growth. But knowing who you are and what you want out of life — and pursuing it passionately — is essential for personal and professional fulfillment.

Over the years, I've witnessed firsthand how companies often settle for average by standardizing their hiring processes and retention programs. I've seen organizations create DEI programs that give the impression they want an inclusive culture but are often tailored to a "type" rather than fostering an environment where people feel they can be their whole selves.

Fortunately, forward-thinking organizations understand that what interests an individual makes them interesting. These YOUnique organizations seek independence and distinct perspectives. They look past large-scale, systematic recruiting processes and prioritize individuality, true diversity, and inclusion. They hire people who, in turn, pledge loyalty because their individual contributions are valued.

Too often, professionals feel pressured to fit into a mold, adjusting their resumes and cover letters to align with perceived expectations. They believe that conforming will enhance their chances of landing a job. Ironically, this strategy often leads to a diluted version of themselves, one that fails to shine in interviews. If you're merely mirroring what others expect, how can you stand out? If you have to change to fit in, do you really want to work there? If you have to be someone different and show up in a way that makes you unhappy, why would you want to stay?

Embracing who you are and who you want to be provides the most freedom to create the career path you want. Don't succumb to the easy road — following others. Find your own path to success. When you do that, your youniqueness will shine in the right organization.

The Fear Factor

I've found that the greatest barrier to reflecting, knowing oneself, being unique, and taking action is fear. The fear that people experience — specifically, the fear of not being accepted for who they are authentically — is something we all grapple with.

Fear can be a formidable barrier, especially when stepping into leadership roles within an organization. Everyone has felt imposter syndrome at some point. It's that nagging fear of being found out, of not being knowledgeable in a certain area.

Often, when we dig deep and uncover aspects of ourselves through assessments that don't align with our self-perception, a new fear emerges: the worry that the organization will suddenly recognize we don't belong in our current position and fire us. There's this overwhelming anxiety that if we start this process of self-discovery and genuine change, it could backfire instead of bringing about the positive outcomes we hope for.

This fear is particularly prevalent among diverse talent. They often feel they need to conform to fit in with everyone else in the organization rather than embracing their uniqueness. As a result, they fear the change itself because they can't envision themselves thriving in the organization as it currently stands. This fear is particularly dangerous. It's a fear that undermines confidence and slows progress both for the individual and the workplace. It creates that self-fulfilling prophecy of lack of representation that continues to manifest, especially in the finance industry.

Imposter syndrome thrives in environments where conformity is encouraged, and for those navigating their careers in finance, this can feel like a trap. There's a pervasive belief that success requires fitting into a narrowly defined mold. Diversity talent, in particular, often feels immense pressure to assimilate, to blend in rather than stand out. This can lead to an overwhelming fear that embracing their authentic selves may result in being judged, sidelined, or overlooked for opportunities. The anxiety of being perceived as different makes many wary of fully embracing their strengths and potential.

The fear of going through an honest assessment process is real. Many hesitate to dive deep into self-reflection, afraid of what they might find. What if an assessment reveals a gap in knowledge or a skill deficiency? What if the organization uses that discovery to justify exclusion or to question their qualifications? These fears are not irrational; they are grounded in the lived experiences of many professionals, especially those in mid-career, who have seen colleagues sidelined after similar revelations.

Adjusting Your Mindset

While fear is valid, it shouldn't hold you back. The reality is that no one has all the answers. Every leader has room to grow, and organizations are starting to see the value in diverse perspectives and experiences.

The real game-changer is shifting your mindset. Instead of being afraid of self-discovery, embrace it as a powerful tool for your personal and professional growth. When you do this, you can turn that fear into a driving force for change and development, the second part of the Alvista Loop Empowerment Process. We'll discuss this further as we explore more about mindset in the next chapter.

CHAPTER 5

Reinforce Your Mindset

"Your life is what your thoughts make it."

– Confucius

Now that we've discussed the importance of knowing your authentic self, take a minute — a time-out — to reflect on thoughts you've had lately. Have you thought about your own happiness, personally and professionally? Have you had self-doubting images lingering in the back of your mind? Have you been worried about a situation? Have you vacillated in making a decision?

The things you dwell on, how you think about situations, and how you view yourself shape so much of your decisions. So many of us don't even realize how much of an impact our day-to-day mindset has on our work environment and productivity. Yet, the things that occupy our minds constantly drive us to or away from meaningful change.

The key to growth and blazing your own trail to success starts with a growth mindset. Unlike a fixed mindset, where you believe that your talents and abilities are innate and unchangeable, a growth mindset is where you know your abilities and skills can constantly improve. You need to have the "yet" mentality. Instead of saying, "I can't do this," embrace, "I can't do this *yet.*"

This growth mindset is paramount in going from insight to impact professionally and personally. In this chapter, we will further explore how you can take your reflections, observe what you want to achieve, and then create and thrive with a growth mindset.

Failure Is the Only Option

Failure. It's a word we've been conditioned to avoid at all costs, especially in competitive industries like finance. I do not doubt that the fear of failure has consumed your mind at some point. We've all experienced it. Yet, the truth is that failure is inevitable. It's part of the process of growth and discovery. To become a leader in finance — or any field, for that matter — you need to fail.

A lot of the fear we discussed in the last chapter comes from a fear of failure, which is why I always say failure is the only option. I truly believe if you're not failing, you're not growing — and if you're not growing, what's the point?

Reinforcing your mindset is all about overcoming fear. Once you've reflected, assessed, and know who you are and the authentic person you want to be, the key is opening yourself up to accepting that and moving forward. It's embracing your growth mindset knowing that although failure is an option, so is success.

I remember running with one of the partners at Arthur Andersen. He wasn't your typical runner. He was built more like a football offensive lineman, but he started a running club at the office and encouraged everyone to join group runs. He even signed us up for fun runs like the Chicago Wacky Snacky 5K each February, which always ended with hot chocolate. Despite his build and pace, he ran marathons, and his determination inspired me to run not just one but three marathons myself.

It wasn't because I loved running or wanted to get in shape. It wasn't that running came easily. It didn't. At 5'3" with short legs and a short stride, I am not built like a runner. However, I am competitive with myself (and others), and I wanted to push myself to see if I could tackle something so challenging. I'd seen my stepdad, Jim, run marathons — he was a cross-country runner in college, so it wasn't surprising that he ran marathons. But this partner and others I saw at the Chicago Marathon were just like me. They didn't have runners' physiques, and they weren't long-distance runners, but they had perseverance and a goal. That's what inspired me.

On my first try, I failed. I got a stress fracture in my foot on a 17-mile training run just four weeks before the marathon. Even though I really wanted to run, it just wasn't feasible. But I wasn't going to let that stop me. I trained harder and more intentionally, determined to run a marathon before my 30th birthday.

And I did. On October 19, 1997, I completed my first marathon—the 20th anniversary Chicago Marathon—in 4 hours and 26 minutes. Me, someone who had never run track, never done cross country, and whose longest run before that was just 20 miles. It was exhilarating, not just to finish, but to know I had accomplished something few people had. I didn't let the prior year's setback stop me from trying again, something that is constantly present when I work with my clients.

One of the biggest barriers professionals face is the fear of failure, and this fear can paralyze you if you let it. Organizations don't want to rock the boat, so they avoid change at any cost. Diverse talent don't want to risk rejection or a bad experience, so they avoid applying to jobs or advocating for positions that seem out of reach or don't seem like a place where they fit in. It's easy to get stuck in a perfectionist mindset, believing every step must be flawless and every decision the right one.

The mindset shift here is important. Sometimes, you will twist an ankle or get a stress fracture in your foot. Keep going. Don't stop just because it becomes hard or you fail on the first try. You know who you are and who you want to be at this point. This is the part of the process where you should explore, push boundaries, and be curious. That's where the growth begins.

Intellectual Curiosity

There's an old saying: "Curiosity killed the cat." It implies curiosity is bad for you and leads to dangerous risk-taking behavior. But this idea of curiosity is pretty outdated — in humans, at least.

Curiosity — the desire to approach novel and challenging ideas and experiences to increase one's knowledge — has long been associated with intellectual pursuit, engagement with the world, memory, and learning. More recently, research suggests curiosity plays a role in our social relationships.

Studies have found that curious people are often viewed in social encounters as more interesting and engaging, and they are more apt to reach out to a wider variety of people. In addition, being curious seems to protect people from negative social experiences, like rejection, which could lead to better connections with others over time.

Effective leaders know how to turn that curiosity inward. They ask themselves hard questions: *How can I be better? What behaviors do I need to adjust to be more effective?* Curiosity, paired with self-reflection, equals direction. The willingness to challenge yourself is what pushes change and achievement.

If you stop being curious, you stop growing — both individually and professionally. And if you're not growing, then your organization isn't going to grow, either. Intellectual curiosity isn't just about gaining technical knowledge. It's also about personal development, especially the softer skills. Sometimes, it's about making behavioral changes, too. When I had to take a hard look at the perceptions others had of me as a "bull in a china shop," I could have been stubborn and not changed. But where would that have gotten me? Not to Managing Director! The ability to shift your mindset and approach things with a curious, open mind leads to success, and it requires a shift in thinking.

Reframing

This shift in thinking comes about as a result of identifying limiting beliefs — like the all-or-none mindset or the thought of "I'm not good enough." Those beliefs can hold you back. We all have limiting beliefs about ourselves. Yet, having an open mindset means reframing those thoughts and looking at things from a different perspective.

This is where the rubber meets the road for most of us.

In an executive coaching session, there are several ways we tackle this reframing process. One of the most common methods is using "if, then" statements. This helps clients explore different outcomes and perspectives. We might also role-play or run through scenarios to reframe conversations or challenge what we believe will happen. These tactics are practical tools that help shift your mindset and break free from the beliefs that keep you stuck. These are the inner narratives that hold you back — things like, "I'm not good enough" or "I can't possibly handle that." When you delve into the *why* behind these narratives and explore ways to remove those obstacles, it opens up a world of possibilities.

For example, using "if, then" statements to reframe means switching from that defeating belief to one of possibility. A very simple instance would be someone thinking, "If I fail, I'll be seen as incompetent." Instead, they could shift their thinking to, "If I fail, I'll learn something valuable that will help me succeed next time." This small change in perspective opens up room for action instead of getting stuck in fear. I could have said, "I can't run a marathon! I've never run anything longer than a 5K." Instead, I decided to say, "I might not finish the marathon, but if I train and put the same grit into it as I did growing up on a cattle farm, I could possibly finish. Besides, if I don't start, I can't finish." That's reframing.

Another example would be role-playing or scenario analysis. In this case, you can walk through conversations or decisions in advance, reframing your mindset for success. For example, if you're dreading a difficult conversation at work, rehearsing the dialogue with a mentor or coach can help you reframe the fear into a learning experience or one of success.

Although these reframing strategies may seem simple, I've found them to be most effective when they're conducted with the support of an outside perspective. Someone who can hold up a mirror and ask the tough questions that you might avoid on your own. These practices, when done effectively, can help take some of the most difficult situations and turn them into opportunities for advancement.

Reframing Your Story

As I've said, my favorite saying is, "Life begins at the end of your comfort zone." When we think about the story of our lives — personal and professional — it's about creating our narratives and sometimes that requires reframing our story.

I remember when I quit my job at Arthur Andersen in 2000 and didn't have a clear plan for what came next. Fear hit me in waves, starting with the terrifying conversation I had to have with my boss, who was also my mentor. Then, the realization I had no solid backup plan. Then, the fear of not being able to pay my mortgage. Finally, the wave of imposter syndrome slammed into me, along with all the others. All of these doubts compounded, building layer upon layer of fear and uncertainty.

That was when I took a time-out. I took a moment, stepped back, got a grip on my fear, and took that time to figure out what I wanted. But it wasn't until I had a pivotal conversation with my stepdad that I began to figure out my next steps. He was the one who held up the mirror and reminded me of my track record. "When have you ever failed at something you set your mind to?" His question forced me to reframe my thinking. Suddenly, what was quickly spiraling into a disaster became an incredible opportunity for me. I didn't just find a way to succeed; that realization also became a turning point in my story.

Life begins at the end of your comfort zone.

It was in that conversation where I thought, "Okay, if I can be successful here, why not stretch and aim for my ultimate goal?" That's when I pivoted directly into the finance industry. Instead of staying on the periphery as a tax consultant, I moved into the heart of the industry — working with almost the exact same clients but advising them in a completely different way. And from there, I was able to grow a profitable division.

I was able to reframe because I recognized the fears and doubts that were building on each other and made the choice to view them through a different lens. My own executive coach — my stepdad — helped me to achieve that. He had pivoted careers many times and was not only a life-guiding force for me but also showed me how reframing a situation could lead to failure or success, something I like to share with my clients.

While this experience may look different for every individual and organization, it's possible to change a seemingly bad situation into something great. In doing so, you open yourself up to growth, new opportunities, and ultimately, a path to success.

The Origin of Growth

The reality is that fear will always be there — and that's okay. Embrace it. Accepting failure as an option, instead of fearing it, frees you from getting stuck and stagnating. It encourages curiosity, openness, and a willingness to reframe your thinking. Growth doesn't happen when we are always hitting our targets or sticking to the strategies we know. Life — growth — takes place when we step out of our comfort zones and risk failure. This is what opens you up to the process and strengthens your mindset.

It's in those moments when you stretch beyond what you believe is possible that real growth happens. It's that point in the empowerment process when you can optimize on your reflection, insight, and growth mindset. It's when you take action.

CHAPTER 6

Lights, Camera, Action

"Every action you take is a vote for the type of person you wish to become."

– James Clear

Have you ever been behind the scenes of a movie? Or watched a documentary about how a TV show was made? There's a lot of work that goes on in the background. Props, costumes, staging, camera placement — these things are all assigned, coordinated, and prepped in advance for the successful shooting of the scenes. All of this preparation builds up to that exciting moment when the director says, "Action!"

I've discovered that we can often get caught up with all the preparation. We can conduct dozens of assessments, and take time-outs to reflect and know ourselves. We can establish the right mindset, conquer our fears, and be ready to fail. However, if we don't take the right action, none of the preparation matters.

When it comes to making real change and achieving success, the most important step is taking action. But let's be honest: taking action is hard. Often, we get stuck in the planning phase, waiting for the "right moment." Yet, no change happens without movement. If you want to grow, you've got to propel yourself forward, no matter how daunting it seems.

Does the Goal Inspire You?

Understanding what motivates you to change is key; it often boils down to your goals and knowing who you want to become, what you want to achieve — and why.

When working with clients, I often ask, "What is our goal?" The answers I receive vary. They might want to change a habit or grow as professionals. Once we've identified their goal, the next step is to make sure we have the right mindset, and then figure out how to act on it, knowing we're committed to making it happen.

Inspiration plays a significant role in this process. Sometimes, it comes from others who motivate us to take action; other times, that inspiration comes from within ourselves. Action stems from knowing your goal and feeling inspired to achieve it.

What do *you* want? What is the specific goal that drives you? Whether it's advancing in your finance career, breaking through leadership barriers, or balancing professional growth with your personal life, that goal needs to be crystal clear. Knowing what's important to you is the foundation for every action you take.

Once you've identified your goal, ask yourself: *Why does this matter?* Knowing the "why" behind your goal propels you to take action. For many mid-career professionals, especially women balancing a variety of roles, this "why" can come from different places. Maybe it's the desire to set an example for other women in finance. Or, maybe it's the realization that staying comfortable means stagnating, while stepping out of your comfort zone will lead to real growth.

Often, what pushes us forward is inspiration. Sometimes, it's someone we admire — a mentor or a trailblazer in the industry. We see what they've achieved, and it sparks something inside us. Other times, the inspiration comes from within. We recognize that the only person who can truly change our trajectory is ourselves. So, we stop waiting for the perfect conditions and start making moves.

The point is that once that spark of inspiration hits, you have to act on it. And that's where the challenge lies. How do you go from feeling motivated to actually doing something about it? This is where many people falter, not because they don't know their goals but because they're unsure how to turn that vision into action.

Taking Small Steps

When we think about achieving our goals, we often imagine grand leaps forward. However, I usually encourage clients to break the big picture down into smaller, more manageable steps. If your goal is to lead a team at your finance firm, what does that require? Maybe it's developing leadership skills through training or taking the initiative to lead a project. Perhaps it's finding a mentor who's already in a leadership position and learning from their experiences. These are much smaller steps that lead to your greater goal.

Remember the marathon I mentioned earlier? Successfully completing the challenge wasn't just about overcoming failure. I had a clear goal: I wanted to run a marathon before I turned 30. Now, anyone who has been both an investment banker and a tax consultant knows that you don't have a lot of extra time for training. So, I had to set bite-sized goals, like running 2 to 3 miles a day plus one longer run on the weekend just so I could accomplish the goal.

What I discovered was that breaking it down and following a structured 16-week plan made all the difference. I created an action plan that wasn't daunting week by week, and it made me commit to how much I would run each week. I found accountability through my friend, Leslie, who would check in with me each weekend to see how I had trained that week.

When I got that stress fracture in my foot after 12 weeks of training, it was a setback that made me question whether I really wanted to achieve this goal. But I'm not a quitter, so I decided to train again the following year.

In that second year, I followed the same 16-week plan, and I was in a bit better shape. I ended up finishing my first marathon in just under 4 and a half hours, exactly as I had hoped. Through the small steps, an action plan, and an accountability partner, I turned a 26.2-mile journey into one step at a time and a medal at the end of a very long race.

Even when you have identified your goal and acted on it, you may find obstacles keeping you down. That's why being truly inspired by your goal is so important. You need that drive to continue to take action when you're confronted with difficulty.

What I loved most about completing that marathon was that my success inspired Leslie to run her own marathon. For me, action is about overcoming fear and taking small steps — just like a marathoner does — toward achieving that long-term goal. And hopefully, through that journey, you can inspire others along the way. Remember: *Be inspired. Be inspiring.*

Another example of taking action even in the most tumultuous times happened in January 2015. Since being promoted to Managing Director at BNP Paribas in 2012, I had continued to build my global teams and had become an integral part of the implementation of Dodd-Frank and the Volcker Rule. I was flying back and forth from Montana to NYC every other week and, by all accounts, was making a true difference in the professional development of my team members and implementing regulatory change across tens of thousands of accounts.

However, on Friday, January 30, 2015, after flying back to Montana late the night before, my boss called and fired me. He said it was due to inappropriate personal actions that had taken place earlier in the week when out with colleagues. Upon digging deeper, what was true was that I had been drugged at a bar when out with these colleagues who I had trusted. Instead of the firm doing their due diligence and using the toxicology report that was provided as evidence, they fired me. Now, New York is an at-will employment state so they can fire anyone, anytime. However, at that moment, I had to make a hard decision. Was I going to let BNP Paribas get away with not supporting me as an employee, or was I going to take action? Well, if you've learned anything about me so far, you know I take action!

I spent the next 3 months dealing with lawyers and confronting colleagues who I thought would support me while realizing they had their own self-preservation at the top of their "to-do" list. I also took time to figure out what I wanted to do next. I took time to spend with my kids and even went to Spring Training in Arizona, all as part of another time-out. I could have been a "deer in headlights" and paralyzed by what had happened, allowing despair and feelings of betrayal to win. Instead, I reflected. I reframed the situation and adopted a growth mindset. And, I acted. I decided to pivot careers at that point and spend more time on my family while creating a new business and finance program at Amherst College, where I worked with Millennials and Gen Zers, placing them in the finance industry for a decade. That ability to take time to know what I wanted at that point in my personal and professional life allowed me to pivot my career and develop even more skills and knowledge that have added to the experience and knowledge I provide to my talent development programs and executive coaching clients.

So, again, I ask, what do *you* want? What is your goal? What small steps can you take to achieve that goal?

Once you've identified those small steps, you simply have to consistently work at them until you're successful. Once you've successfully achieved these changes, you just have to keep doing what you did to get there. That's the challenging part, however. To create sustainable change and get repeat results, you'll have to establish powerful habits.

CHAPTER 7

Make It a Habit

"Motivation gets you going, but discipline keeps you growing. That's the Law of Consistency."

– John Maxwell

Let's talk about making change a habit. Taking action is an important part of the empowerment and growth process. Action brings about change. Yet, change without consistency will eventually undo itself. Change and success become repeatable and sustainable once you turn action into a habit. It might sound redundant, but the heart of consistency lies in holding yourself accountable and letting others hold you accountable, too. This way, you create change through consistent action, and your actions become habits that create a loop of change, growth, and success.

This process of creating a habit is embedded in the Alvista Loop Empowerment Process. You need to:

- **Listen** to yourself and know who you are and who you want to be.

- **Observe** what others see and what you see in yourself.
- **Optimize** your growth through reframing and finding the right mindset.
- **Propel** yourself into action and make it consistent.

This is an infinity loop that allows you continuous growth and empowerment — empowering yourself and others.

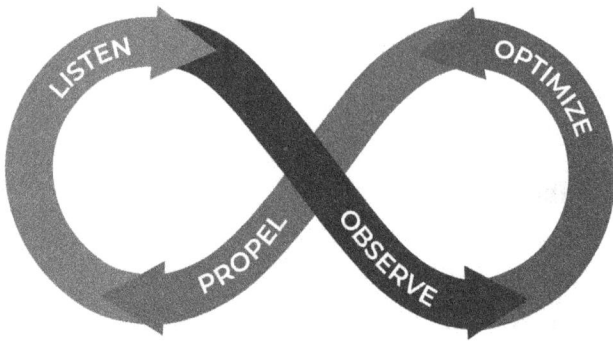

Making Change Repeatable

As an executive coach, I help my clients act *and* create habits to put themselves on a continuous loop of growth, improvement, and success. We collaborate to identify what inspires them — their goals — and then create action steps that take them from insight to impact. Here's the catch: if you don't recognize the rewards you've earned and celebrate those wins, you're less likely to keep the habit alive. You need that pat on the back, that acknowledgment from others, to stay motivated and consistent.

You need the right people in your life to acknowledge you and help hold you accountable. For example, with my clients, one of the things we may work on is setting goals around behavior and implementing steps to hold themselves accountable. By way of illustration, I had a client who was very talkative and oftentimes talked over others, not letting them finish their thoughts. We created a plan to help him stop talking over people in meetings by putting a post-it note on his agenda at the meeting to remind him to allow others to complete their thoughts.

Sure, you can work on building that habit on your own, but the real change happens when you go to a colleague, direct report, or boss and say, "Hey, I'm working on this behavior. Please hold me accountable and let me know if you see me improving." That outside accountability makes a huge difference. That's exactly what my client did and he was rewarded by his colleague who acknowledged when he allowed it to happen and when he didn't. Eventually, the ability to let others complete their thoughts became the norm instead of the exception and he was recognized by others as being a better listener and leader.

The moment someone else recognizes your effort and acknowledges that you're improving, it reinforces your commitment. That recognition drives consistency, and the more often you practice it, the more it becomes second nature. What started as a change becomes a habit, something you no longer have to think about.

But there's always some risk when it comes to change. You can set your goal, keep an open mindset, take action, and create a habit, but there's still risk. You can still fall short. Just like when I didn't finish the marathon the first time around, failure is part of the process. But you take that risk for the reward to happen — just like everyone in the finance industry does. They're willing to take risks because they know it leads to big payoffs, both financially and personally.

It's no different when you're going through a change process. Whether it's developing a new habit or pushing yourself toward a goal, you're taking a risk for the potential reward. That's what the Alvista Loop Empowerment Process is about — being willing to take that leap, knowing what you want, making the necessary changes, building habits, reaping the rewards, and creating a continuous cycle of growth and improvement.

A good example of when I utilized the Alvista Loop Empowerment Process, although it was not named at the time, was when I made a change that, through habit, generated success. It was first developed in the Summer of 2008. I was leading the efforts to transition 695 clients from Bank of America to BNP Paribas as part of the sale of the prime services division. I was responsible for motivating the account representatives to work with their clients to ensure all the paperwork was completed to effect the transfer, which was to occur on September 30, 2008, the height of the financial crisis. My biggest challenge was effectively communicating the client transition status to the management of both sides of the transaction, Bank of America and BNP Paribas. Each party had its own goals for the transition, and I needed to ensure both sides had 100% of the information in a way that was complete and convincing.

To achieve this, I created a weekly standardized summary report that reflected the current status and our progress toward our goal — 100% of clients transferred to BNP Paribas. That level of consistent, clear communication, I learned, was one of the reasons management at BNP Paribas felt secure in their decision to purchase the prime services division. This might seem like a small thing to do or an obvious action plan, but it had an outsized impact on my career trajectory. Throughout my career, I've used a similar communication strategy to create effective communication, whether it's the client updates as the Head of Client Integration at BNP Paribas or the weekly *Careers in Finance* newsletters at Amherst College. It's the habit of consistent, effective communication that has set me up for career success and to gain a reputation for effective implementation. This habit of clear communication is also a reason clients find my executive coaching sessions so impactful.

The 24-Hour Rule

I was not always an effective communicator. Remember, many thought of me as the bull in the china shop. I was also considered reactionary. I had to learn to curb my initial reaction and tendency to speak without thinking. Early in my career, when people did things I thought were stupid, I would immediately want to fire off an email telling them everything they did wrong and demanding they fix it right away. The perfectionist in me would come through in my writing. As you can imagine, this led to some regrettable moments.

Years ago, I read a story about how Benjamin Franklin wrote an angry letter to a friend of his in the British Parliament, but instead of sending it, he stuffed it into a drawer. The simple act of writing what he wished to say satisfied his urge to unload a tirade of venom. (Several other notable historical figures have also famously made use of the angry, unsent letter, including Abraham Lincoln and Mark Twain.)

So I created what I call "Stephanie's 24-Hour Rule."

Step one is simple: Write the email. Write your thoughts and grievances. Get everything out. Vent on paper or in the draft, unload all the frustration, and say exactly what you're feeling.

But the key? Don't hit send. Let it sit for 24 hours. The next day, with a cooler head, revisit it. Most of the time, it ends up reworded to be less reactionary and more constructive. Sometimes it doesn't even get sent.

> **The 24-Hour Rule**
>
> Try it yourself. Whenever someone says or does something that triggers you, take a deep breath and pull out a pen and piece of paper. From my own experience, the act of ripping up your letter allows the tension to dissipate further. It's a symbolic act of telling yourself that the thing no longer bothers you.

While I can't claim I've never broken this rule — we've all hit send on that impulsive message! — I've significantly reduced those moments. The 24-hour rule has allowed me to create a more positive communication style that fosters collaboration rather than conflict. It's become a habit — I just don't send angry emails anymore.

Our habits have the power to change our environments and workplaces. Think about how my new habit shifted the workplace culture. Which version of me would *you* rather approach? Annoyed, angry Stephanie? Or level-headed, constructive Stephanie?

Whatever the change you want to implement, you'll have to set up a system to make it into a habit. Whether the change is only you as an individual or an organization-wide adjustment, habits take time and effort.

The Importance of People

Habits are hard to develop on your own. You may be able to start them, but creating sustainable change isn't an easy thing for one person to do. Throughout my life, I've always had people who have encouraged me to grow and develop positive habits. The people you choose to acknowledge you and hold you accountable are a key part of your change journey. That's one of the reasons I started Alvista Loop. It's a way to help hold others accountable for the change they want for themselves. It's also, by extension, a way to be a catalyst for others to change. As we'll see in the next chapter, just like your support people empower you, you also have the ability to empower others.

CHAPTER 8

Empower Yourself to Empower Others

"To empower yourself you must find your purpose. To empower others is to live your purpose."

— Jen Groover

Throughout this book, I've acknowledged various people who have influenced my journey. I've mentioned colleagues, family, friends, and mentors. There's no way to undergo a journey of change without bringing other people along. You need them to hold you accountable, encourage you, advise you, and point out when you're making poor decisions.

The law of conservation of energy states that, "Energy can neither be created nor destroyed; rather, it can only be transformed or transferred from one form to another." For one object to gain energy, it must get that energy from something else. Similarly, to empower other people to create change and reach their goals, you must be empowered yourself.

Your Personal Board of Directors

Success, whether personal or professional, is a collective effort supported by a group of individuals who inspire, challenge, and guide us. I like to think of these vital players as my "personal Board of Directors." This group can include anyone from family members to mentors and friends, each bringing their unique perspective and influence.

One of the most significant influences in my life has been my mom. She served as a cornerstone of my personal board, consistently holding me accountable. When I was cutting corners or not being my best self, she was there to call me out, and when I needed support or encouragement, she was right there, cheering me on. My stepdad, Jim, joined her in that circle. He also gave me guidance and imparted wisdom that shaped who I am today, especially from a business perspective.

A personal Board of Directors can look different for everyone. For me, it extends beyond family. I have cherished relationships with mentors who have provided invaluable insights and guidance throughout my career. I have friends who have been my bedrock through good and bad times. I have former colleagues who have gone in different directions but are still a sounding board when I need to talk. And, I have my husband, Chris, who not only supports my professional aspirations but also brings a unique perspective that challenges my thinking.

These are the individuals who hold up a mirror, allowing me to acknowledge my hard work and accomplishments. They remind me that success isn't just about reaching a destination; it's about recognizing the journey and the effort it took to get there. This acknowledgment empowers me to continue striving for more while empowering others along the way. So, how do you assemble your personal Board of Directors? Start by identifying the people in your life who inspire and empower you. Who challenges you to be better? Who celebrates your successes, big or small? These individuals could be colleagues, family members, friends, or even acquaintances who have impacted your life in meaningful ways.

Don't take this action lightly. Our Board of Directors shapes who we are. A great board can help us harness our strengths and put them to use. Great boards help us recognize our weaknesses, work on them, and point us in directions that minimize those weaknesses while showcasing our strengths. A poor Board of Directors is one we believe has our best interest at heart: those who we think know us, but are not willing to be by your side when you need them. They are the cowards that run from a fight rather than stand by your side. Avoid creating a poor Board of Directors; it is a waste of time and energy and can also be detrimental.

Once you've identified your great Board of Directors, cultivate those relationships. Share your goals, challenges, and successes. Open the lines of communication. Ask for their input and advice, and be receptive to their feedback. Your personal Board of Directors is your sounding board, your trusted advisors who will be authentic and honest with you because they have your best interest at heart.

Your Organizational Support System

When it comes to work, I've always focused on finding team members and leaders who challenge me, and not just agree with everything I say. I believe it's important to surround yourself with colleagues who push you beyond your limits. These people gave me the latitude to take risks and provided the resources to make those endeavors possible. By doing this, I wasn't just empowered to accomplish whatever task was at hand; I was also able to empower my own team members. I wanted others to see that they, too, could accomplish their goals — whether as a woman in finance trying to rise through the ranks or a Gen Xer trying to explain to "Boomers" how we get things done in this new technological era.

Conversely, it's just as crucial to recognize those who want to take away your power. There are often people who suck the energy out of the room. If you want to keep your energy, you have to identify who they are and remove them from your immediate circle of colleagues — those who truly empower you. If not, those people will drain your ability to accomplish things.

A great example of this happened when I was very early in my career at Bank of America. I trusted a certain colleague with a lot of information — someone I counted on as a reliable partner. But as often happens in the finance industry, I got stabbed in the back. This person took my ideas, presented them to my boss's boss, and took all the credit for my work. It was a turning point for me. I learned the hard way that I needed to be more selective about who I trusted and who really had my back. I had to decide if I wanted to be a person who trusted someone until they broke that trust or a person who only gave their trust once it was earned.

At that moment, I had to empower myself again. Not only did I have to tell my boss what happened, but I also had to go to my boss's boss to make it clear that those ideas were mine. Despite what I said in the previous chapter about being forthright, speaking up for myself was not the easiest thing to do, especially early on in my career, but it was a necessary lesson in owning my work and protecting my voice. I took that lesson and applied it throughout the rest of my career. I've also found that the experience gave me great insight into working with coaching clients who face similar situations, especially clients seeking ways to find their voice in an oftentimes "loud" industry.

I learned that establishing an organizational support system that genuinely empowers you requires both diligence and discernment. You have to create a network of individuals who encourage growth and challenge you to excel. And once you have your network, you can become a beacon of empowerment for others.

Empowering Others

Empowering others is a key part of not just my work but my life. I truly believe the more people pour into me, the more I should be willing to pour into others. Especially those who may not have historically been able to get the same support. It's my pay-it-forward mentality.

I've always been a big proponent of advancing the cause of women in finance throughout my career. Specifically, when I made Managing Director at BNP Paribas, I was recognized as one of the future women leaders in the organization. I was one of four women in New York and among 20 women globally who were part of the newly created Women's Leadership Initiative. This initiative was designed to recognize up-and-coming senior female leaders in the organization.

In the New York office, the four of us took this as an opportunity to really think about how we could change the narrative for women at BNP Paribas. We created the Women's Leadership Initiative speaker series, where we invited clients and the women in the organization to listen to keynote speakers talk about how women can make a meaningful impact in a male-dominated industry. Our very first speaker, Madeleine Albright, the first female Secretary of State, really set the tone. Her presence in front of a room full of financiers highlighted how women could influence not just industries but entire mindsets.

From that, we started to see results. During the next promotion cycle, more women were being recognized for promotion — from where they were to where they could be. The Women's Leadership Initiative was doing exactly what it was supposed to do — empowering women to ask for promotions and feel comfortable taking that next step in their careers.

I remember one young woman who worked on a different team from mine. Shortly after Madeleine Albright's talk, she found out she was pregnant. We worked together to figure out how she would tell her male boss — a conversation that, unfortunately, was more difficult than it should have been. But what stood out even more was that as she was preparing to return to work from her maternity leave, we realized there was no lactation room on our floor. This was a clear sign that the workplace wasn't set up to fully support women. As a member of the Women's Leadership Initiative, I was able to help her advocate for her needs and to make changes that truly impacted women in the office, ensuring they had the resources they needed to balance their careers and their families.

This initiative was a huge step forward. It empowered women to ask for what they needed, whether it was a promotion or something as basic as a lactation room. It helped women feel confident to take the next step in their careers and make real changes in the organization.

This is the essence of what I mean by empowering yourself so you can empower others. Just as the Arthur Andersen partner empowered me to run my marathon, and Jim empowered me to look in the mirror and see who I truly was, I was able to empower another woman in the industry to speak up and advocate for changes, not just for herself but for others as well.

Empowering Change

By now, you should understand how essential support systems are for making the process of empowerment work effectively. Over the next few chapters, we'll be looking at bigger topics that are directly relevant to the finance industry and, more specifically, your organization. Empowering change requires identifying the unique challenges and using specialized strategies to navigate them successfully.

The process of empowerment is meant to lead to meaningful change. Now, we'll explore how that change can be applied within specific subsets of the finance industry and, ultimately, how we can position organizations to attract, grow, and retain early-career talent.

CHAPTER 9

Attracting Early-Career Talent

"The only limit to the height of your achievement is the reach of your dreams and your willingness to work hard for them."

– Michelle Obama

As we mentioned in the earlier chapters, most organizations, especially in the financial services industry, may be able to attract the right talent, but they often fall short once those people are on board. They'll give new hires a little training — maybe a few weeks — and then send them off to work, relying on management and team members to provide on-the-job training.

The problem is that this approach doesn't work well, especially with early-career talent. Gen Zers are digital natives. They've grown up at a peak of technological innovation, where information is immediately accessible and social media increasingly ubiquitous. They are pragmatic and financially minded, shaped by the financial crisis and watching their parents take huge financial hits during the Great Recession. Having witnessed their parents' struggles, Gen Zers are driven to seek security even as they constantly balance life and work in a way previous generations didn't.

Many organizations fail to properly prepare these employees to be successful on the job. While they might provide technical skills training, they often neglect the soft skills these young professionals aren't learning anywhere else — skills critical for long-term success. Organizations aren't recognizing these employees' desire to learn and grow holistically and find security in their organizations. They must start to think differently, outside their comfort zones, to attract, grow, and retain their diverse talent.

If organizations aren't onboarding talent correctly or focusing only on their pragmatic, technology-driven tendencies, retention becomes nearly impossible. Unfortunately, to date, we have not seen finance industry firms truly grasp the need to change their early-career talent onboarding and training which has further exacerbated the two-and-out philosophy prevalent in the Millennial generation. They come in, spend two years gaining skills, and then move on — whether it's to another job or to take a break.

For Millennials, there's even a trend, often referred to as FIRE (**F**inancial **I**ndependence, **R**etire **E**arly), where people work just long enough to be able to stop working. If they need to, they will then return to the workforce to do it all over again.

This short-term mentality damages organizations because it prevents them from retaining valuable talent. Successful companies understand that if they onboard new hires properly and give them compelling reasons to stay, they'll avoid the constant cycle of hiring and rehiring, saving both time and money.

The Alvista Loop LAUNCH Program

The LAUNCH program was conceived after a decade of experience working with Millennials and Gen Zers as a career advisor at Amherst College. During that time, I worked with, coached, and advised over 1500 young adults as they navigated finding, starting, and excelling in finance careers. The information I gathered from early-career professionals I placed throughout the finance industry showed a severe lack of attention by finance organizations to seeing the whole individual. Firms would onboard them and provide some technical training but give no training to help them develop the soft skills necessary for growth and professional development. This, in turn, makes the early-career professionals feel not "seen," so they never develop loyalty to the firm and thus leave.

Early-career professionals have a constant refrain — "companies care what I produce but don't care about me." However, these early-career professionals seek organizations that accept them for who they are (authentically) and take the time to develop them holistically. They want to work for an organization that cares enough to develop the whole person, not just provide revenue-producing skills. The LAUNCH program addresses this issue.

This program comprises approximately five small group workshops designed to help early-career talent transition from college to the professional world. We cover everything from strong professional communication skills to personal branding and networking within an organization — skills that are very different from the kind of networking done during recruiting — to navigating multigenerational workforces. The focus is on teaching the soft skills needed to function successfully in the workforce, skills our attendees haven't necessarily gained in a college setting.

After the workshops, we provide one-on-one coaching. This personalized support serves as a sounding board, helping them navigate situations they've never encountered before. For example, I worked with someone about a year into their role who lacked strong communication skills and was struggling with an overbearing boss. Together, we worked on how best to state and deliver a message that would express her frustrations clearly and concisely. In the end, we found the right combination that helped her voice her needs to the manager so that the manager could understand and support her better.

These one-on-one coaching sessions allow us to address specific, timely challenges rather than waiting six months or a year for a formal 360-review process. It also gives early-career professionals immediate guidance and tools to succeed.

The LAUNCH program helps new graduates transition into professional life by providing practical knowledge and essential skills, reducing the risk of career missteps. It also demonstrates to early-career professionals that the company values the development of the whole individual in their personal and professional growth. The LAUNCH program is a great way to help companies attract, develop, and retain diverse talent while leveling the playing field for traditionally underrepresented individuals, who are typically less prepared for the transition to professional life.

What's Possible?

The LAUNCH program is a supplemental personal development initiative designed to empower early-career talent and help them build a successful career within the organization. Every workshop is customized and tailored to the needs of the attendees and their sponsoring organization.

But beyond that, organizations benefit in a variety of meaningful ways. Retention is obviously very important. But even if organizations excel at attracting diverse talent — whether that's diversity of experiences/backgrounds, racial diversity, or gender diversity — the "two-and-out" phenomenon still impacts traditionally underrepresented individuals in the early-career talent pool.

Many of these individuals don't have an even playing field, especially if they're coming from a 1st generation, low-income situation straight out of college. Through the LAUNCH program, we aim to level the playing field. This helps organizations retain diverse talent, which enhances representation within the organization and, in turn, supports the attraction of new talent.

The Challenge With Diverse Talent

Right now, in the financial services industry, organizations are trying to attract diverse talent. However, by grouping everyone together, they do a disservice to traditionally underrepresented individuals because they fail to level the playing field. They often just focus on getting people on board to make their numbers look good. However, there's a real cost to that approach. If you genuinely want to retain diverse talent and create a positive waterfall effect, organizations must buy into and implement effective onboarding strategies.

Building a strong workforce requires intentional effort and action. This generation is more diverse than ever before. In the next chapter, we'll explore what it means to build a multigenerational workforce and a few strategies to go about doing that.

CHAPTER 10

Navigating a Multigenerational Workforce

"We need to remember across generations that there is as much to learn as there is to teach."

– Gloria Steinem

If you've properly positioned your organization to attract early-career talent, you will hopefully face a new problem. With diverse talent usually comes a notable generation gap in your organization's workforce.

The average finance professional is 40+ years old, and that represents some 61% of the finance professional population. However, the industry population spans from Boomers to Gen Zers. When considering these different generations, it's evident that Boomers and Gen Xers grew up without the Internet and AI — technologies that Millennials and Gen Zers rely on daily.

As a result, we've found that communication styles, modes of working, and what's working vary greatly across these generations in the workplace.

The Challenges of Multiple Generations

While variety is great, especially after all the highlights I've presented about empowerment and diversity, connecting multiple generations has, does, and always will provide a unique challenge. As Harvard Business School has stated, "Managing multigenerational workforces is an art in itself. Young workers want to make a quick impact, the middle generation needs to believe in the mission, and the older employees don't like ambivalence."

Organizations face challenges. Oftentimes, they fail to train their senior-level individuals to recognize and adapt their communication and work styles to younger generations. This disconnect can lead to decreased productivity and even result in errors and issues. It can also lead to a misalignment in company values, creating another vicious cycle of lack of representation between those at the company and those the company seeks to attract.

Conversely, if organizations don't help early- and mid-career talent understand what is needed to move forward and grow them in the right way, using what motivates them, they won't stick around. This can lead to a situation where you have a bunch of very seasoned individuals running the show — which is pretty much the status quo. The reality is that different generations see work ethic, productivity, and communication in fundamentally different ways.

Based on the previous chapter and the above comments, you may think I believe younger generations have a commitment problem. You'd be right — sort of. As I've been working with college students and recent Amherst College alumni over the last 10 years, I initially thought that Millennials and Gen Zers didn't seek commitment. They are constantly seeking new adventures, new jobs, and new experiences. However, I've come to realize that it's not that the younger generations are skeptical of commitments, dogma, arbitrary laws, and tradition for the sake of tradition, but instead, they seek a commitment to a truth. A truth that is defined by them. They don't let others define their truth or their life. They define it for themselves.

What I've come to understand after thousands of conversations is that each generation is committed to life, but it's their life and the paths they choose to take for that life that differentiates each generation. They are committed to their truth, their authenticity, and in their own way, they are committed to their life.

The key for organizations is finding what each generation is committed to and helping the other generations learn to value, accept, and respect that commitment. That allows for the authenticity we discussed earlier, and creates a workplace that retains talent.

Working at the Team Level

Facilitating the understanding of multigenerational commitments, values, and practices is not easy, especially when organizational leadership may have a different generational composition than their workforce.

When thinking about a company's demographics, culture, and sometimes its goals, most financial service organizations follow a pyramid structure, with the bulk of employees being early- and mid-career talent. That's why cross-training multigenerational workforces is crucial to not only retention but also attracting and growing that talent.

I've experienced the challenges of a multigenerational workforce firsthand and dealt with the challenges successfully. For example, when I worked at BNP Paribas, I was a member of a professional development board. Our mandate was to enhance the company culture of a one-bank mentality and be innovative in our solutions as part of the "Bank of a Changing World" (the company tagline). We also were asked to identify issues that employees faced and find solutions that would grow and retain the talent.

As a French-headquartered bank with a culturally and generationally diverse workforce, we recognized that the senior leaders and early career talent were struggling to effectively communicate with each other. It wasn't a language barrier but a combination of global culture and multigenerational teams. At times, this led to poor work product, but a majority of the time, it led to early-career talent not feeling heard and deciding to leave. The attrition was an obvious sign we had a problem.

As part of the board, I researched some of the most innovative companies and how they retained and grew multicultural workforces. What we realized was that there wasn't enough training on how to acknowledge and learn how to work collaboratively. That's when we implemented cross-cultural training as well as generation-focused workshops to help each member of a team understand what each member brought to the team, from perspectives to skills to viewpoints. There were discussions and exercises that helped everyone better work with and communicate with each other. These focused measures not only improved overall communication but also productivity and profitability.

This is the same approach we use at Alvista Loop when helping financial institutions better educate their workforce on the nuances of each generation's work and life desires and how to collaboratively work together. We frequently work with multi-generational teams, helping senior-level employees better understand their junior colleagues on both a personal and professional level and vice versa. We discuss their communication styles and how to adjust to one another. Many times, we'll conduct workshops for senior-level individuals to help them understand and adapt to younger generations while also implementing the LAUNCH program (see previous chapter) that includes a workshop on collaborating across multigenerational workforces. A common example we address is the misconception that if someone has earbuds in, they're not working. We make sure Boomers and Gen Xers know that just because they're listening to music doesn't mean they aren't productive, and we make sure younger generations understand the importance of being accessible and not isolating.

A lot of challenges can be solved through both communication and understanding. Much of what we do is focused on re-educating across generations to help them function better as a team. The amazing thing is how success in one team can create a ripple effect throughout the organization. For example, a successful team dynamic born out of a workshop may lead to individual coaching, and when team members leave for other companies, they often take these successful strategies with them, further spreading the positive effects. This ripple effect can even extend to client relationships, especially when client-facing teams improve their internal dynamics, positively impacting how they interact with clients.

In fact, I once worked with an organization where most of the members were older Gen Xers and Boomers, but they were increasingly having to interact with younger generation clients. The team struggled to communicate effectively because they weren't used to the different styles and expectations of this younger group. So, we focused on helping these teams improve their communication, not just internally but also with their clients, to bridge that generational gap. This resulted in better client relationships and increased revenue.

In our workshops, I will often connect how we can better communicate with our multigenerational workforces and clients with how we communicate within our families. The simple ability to relate communication styles like you would with family members is something that everyone can understand. A great example was when I was working with the head of a division at an investment bank who was a Boomer. When he would speak to the hundreds of multigenerational colleagues in his division town hall, he struggled to connect, especially with the younger Gen Xers and Millennials. His communication style didn't connect with the analysts and associates he needed to motivate to get the strategic goals of the organization implemented. The problem was his delivery and style.

He had three daughters who were all Millennials. We did a lot of work on how he would communicate the same information to his daughters. We talked about what he said versus what his daughters would "hear." We worked for about four weeks on how to adjust his communication style, including content and delivery, and we did a lot of role-playing and practicing to perfect the delivery. The next town hall presentation he gave was much better received due to the change in his tone for the presentation and the examples he used. The feedback he received was positive and many commented that they were energized to move forward and implement the strategy.

Building Across Generations

It's very easy for one generation to write off another as "entitled," "out of touch," or even "irrelevant." Yet, each generation brings a unique and important perspective to an organization.

Millennials are now taking over middle management. This group grew up during pivotal moments, like terrorist attacks and the Great Recession, which shaped them in unexpected ways. They bring a desire to focus on connection and collaboration and seek meaning in their work. They understand the importance of drawing together to tackle a difficult problem. Gen Xers, on the other hand, are a different kind of connecting generation. They came into adulthood during the rise of the internet and had to constantly adapt to new technologies, making them incredibly versatile.

Each generation carries its own strengths and weaknesses. When organizations can recognize and direct those energies, communication improves, and so does the work product. Teams begin to grow individually, but more importantly, that growth is translating into better team dynamics, increased effectiveness, and higher performance. This growth expands to the division, and ultimately, the entire organization benefits from improved efficiency and profitability — assuming you're running things correctly. As the team grows, the division grows, and so does the organization. Creating well-functioning teams creates a continuous loop of improvement and growth for the organization. Through creating insight into each workforce generation, the Alvista Loop Empowerment Process creates infinite impact.

A New Generation of Women

As much discussion as we've had about generations and learning to listen, there's one population that is still struggling to be heard. Women across all generations are still fighting to use their voices. In the next chapter, we'll look at why this population is vital to organizational growth and how you can better draw on their unique talents.

CHAPTER 11

Empowering Women to Empower Your Organization

"I love to see a young girl go out and grab the world by the lapels. Life's a bitch. You've got to go out and kick ass."
— Maya Angelou

As a woman in the finance industry for over three decades, I've often been asked what the greatest issues are for women in finance. Some people want to know how they can increase their diversity. Others are looking for a better understanding of their workforce and how to support women. Still, others are just curious about my thoughts and experiences. When I think about the biggest problem for women in finance, it's simple: there just aren't enough of them.

Wonder Women

The lack of female role models is a major issue, especially in the finance industry. Women need to see a variety of role models showing that they can take different paths in the industry and find their own path to success. They need to see people who choose to be married, choose to remain single, have kids, and focus on a family, or forgo kids to seek other paths. Regardless of the path they choose, women need to be supported by other women, men, and organizations. The industry needs to include diversity at the top, with women representing all of these different life choices. They need more women role models that I think of as Wonder Women — those that exemplify a culture we want — women who are empowered, courageous, wise, diverse, resilient, and strong.

I once caught up with one of the most infectious leaders I know. She's been in the financial services industry for over 30 years and developed one of the most impactful, inclusive cultures at her firm. During that conversation, my friend recounted an amazing story of two Wonder Women.

Two incredible Black women in their mid-twenties were featured in a company-wide video conference that was seen by over 800 people in their organization. Galvanized by the Black Lives Matter movement, these young women initiated a forthright discussion about their lives and their experiences. They talked about their personal experiences (one single and one married with children), and they discussed their professional journeys, including the challenges they faced and the support they received. Moreover, they talked candidly about how others in their lives helped shape those experiences. Their goal was to better educate their colleagues. I still get goosebumps thinking about how these young women of color felt so themselves at this organization and so empowered that they were able to create a dynamic discussion and enhance the lives of so many. They were the rock in a body of water that created a ripple effect of knowledge and understanding throughout their firm and the finance industry.

These are the kinds of role models women need to see. But more importantly, these women were able to act because they felt empowered by their organization to do so. Too many organizations struggle with how to treat women in the workplace. Men, and even some women, often treat a subset of women differently, reinforcing outdated cultural norms instead of empowering them to be themselves. There needs to be a cultural shift where men actively support women in ways that help them succeed — empowering them to empower themselves rather than making exceptions or casually tailoring special programs. This tendency to "customize" creates a culture of disparity instead of one that promotes equality and growth.

Similarly, women need to support other women regardless of their personal choices. As Madeleine Albright once said, "There's a special place in hell for women who don't help other women."

WiFi Womentorship

In every aspect of my life, I've sought to support and empower other women. In my 20s while working at Arthur Andersen, I was a volunteer basketball coach for 8th-grade girls on the West Side of Chicago near the Cook County hospital (not the greatest area of town at the time). I sought to teach them the skills to succeed on the court, but more importantly, I served as a role model of what hard work, dedication, and aspirations could create. I wanted (and I hope I succeeded) to show how a girl who grew up on a cattle farm in Oklahoma and adapted through a divorce and multiple moves could use sports and the power of teammates as a stabilizing influence to become a successful professional.

In my 30s, I sought to become a role model to women at Bank of America and BNP Paribas. As someone who married at 33 and then at 35 and 36 had kids, all while managing teams and taking on more and more responsibility and ultimately, climbing to Managing Director at 41 years old, I sought to hire more women on my teams and be a role model. I wanted them to see a path they could follow while supporting those who chose different personal paths.

In my 40s and early 50s, I've used my experience and influence to help make organizations and the finance industry become more inviting for women. Whether it was launching the Women in Finance organization on the Amherst College campus or sharing my experiences and insights to create an open forum for discussion, I've sought to open others' eyes to the possibility of their careers and personal lives within the finance industry.

My lifelong pursuit of being an example for others led to the creation of numerous Women in Finance initiatives at Bank of America, BNP Paribas, and now at Alvista Loop, called WiFi Womentorship. We've created initiatives to connect and engage women from diverse backgrounds. Quarterly dinners are a key part of what we do, held in select cities and bringing together women at various stages of their careers in finance. At each dinner, there's a central topic for discussion, but the main goal is to create a space where women can network, share advice, and build a broader support system. It's about connecting women who have faced or are facing similar challenges and allowing them to learn from each other. It has its own momentum and is creating an even more powerful ripple effect.

What I love most is the multigenerational aspect — women at different career phases helping one another. We also bring women from different organizations into the mix, which is crucial. While internal affinity groups, like women's or mom groups, are great, they often exist within the same organizational culture, with the same bosses and policies, which limits honest conversation.

Gathering women from different companies serves two purposes. First, it shows that many challenges are common across organizations, helping women feel less isolated. Second, it provides fresh perspectives from women who've successfully navigated similar situations, allowing them to share solutions that others can bring back to their own workplaces. It's like a petri dish for mentorship, fostering discussions that can lead to real changes in organizations simply by bringing diverse voices together. The ultimate hope is that each woman can take what she gains in these discussions and then impact others in their organization — expanding the ripple effect.

Wifi Womentorship

If you have women on your team, consider connecting them to this opportunity. It will broaden their exposure, provide a strong support network, and empower them. It's a great way to show your team how much you value and invest in their growth! You can find more information by visiting us directly at https://alvistaloop.com/wifi-womentorship/.

Real Conversations

I've always thrived in group settings, but I've also gained enormous growth from one-on-one discussions. At times, these more individualized opportunities have allowed me to explore and consider options in a more intimate setting. That's one of the reasons I've become an executive coach. Through my one-on-one coaching, I'm able to help others, especially women, consider and explore their options and create action steps to achieve their goals. One-on-one coaching is all about being a sounding board, using my personal experiences as a woman in the industry to help navigate issues. Sure, we often cover the basics like work-life balance, having kids, and all that — but it goes deeper. A lot of the time, we're discussing how to have more presence in an organization and how to feel confident enough to ask for what you want.

A great example of this is the multiple conversations I've had with women about negotiating for a higher salary or bonus, especially since women continue to be underpaid by an average of 15% from their male counterparts. We all know there is a pay disparity between the genders, but what I've experienced first-hand is the fact that women don't ask for more money, but men do. When I ran a global team at BNP Paribas that consisted of 60% men and 40% women at various stages in their careers (analysts, associates, VPs), I met with them individually to give them their annual bonus numbers. What always struck me was the fact that the men were always willing to challenge the number given and ask why they weren't getting a higher amount while the women said, "Thanks." I hated that the women didn't have the confidence the way the men did. It was an opportunity to coach them, which I did. I've continued to try and build confidence and presence for a new generation of women in finance through my executive coaching at Alvista Loop and my career advising at Amherst College, where I constantly coach women to ask for higher salaries, higher bonuses, etc. As I tell them, even if you are told "no," you are setting a precedent that you understand your value proposition to the organization.

A lot of my coaching is sharing these kinds of experiences, reminding women: if you don't ask, you don't get. And really, what's the worst that can happen? We also focus on presence, confidence, and speaking up in the right way. I even share how to apply the "24-hour rule" I explained in Chapter 6 to help navigate tricky situations.

For me, this all ties back to the importance of empowering others, just as I was empowered. Each empowered woman can then go on to empower more women and so forth. These real conversations are a key part of the Alvista Loop process and how we continue to create lasting and sustainable change within organizations.

The Future for Women

Have you ever heard of Lucy Stone? She was the first woman in America to keep her own name after getting married. She was the first woman from Massachusetts to earn a bachelor's degree. She was also the first American to become a full-time lecturer for women's rights, mobilizing countless supporters and converting adversaries to join the movement.

She was an early advocate of antislavery and women's rights. She led the suffragist movement and paved the way for me and countless other women to vote. She started a movement that included great women of history like Amelia Earhart and Georgia O'Keefe, as well as more recent influencers like Beyoncé, Sheryl Sandberg, and Sarah Jessica Parker. She inspired so many women to be more than the "appendages of society." She is the ultimate role model, inspiring women to be equal among men and blazing a trail for so many others to follow.

Modeling is an extremely important part of effective empowerment. The truth is that having more women role models, both within your organization and externally, is essential for creating the true diversity this industry craves — and, more importantly, that the clients finance companies serve are demanding. There's a reason policies exist to push for 30% women on corporate boards — because it's proven that companies with more women at the top are more profitable.

Clients don't want to work with financial institutions that lack female representation in leadership. The future we need is one where there are more senior-level women, across all life choices, who early-career talent can look up to, emulate, and follow. We need representation.

CHAPTER 12

Empowering an Industry

"The ultimate use of power is to empower others."

– William Glasser

I mentioned earlier in this book that the finance industry moves capital from those who have it to those who need it. It's the lifeblood of our economy. Without a diverse, well-rounded, and culturally rich industry, we'll continue to see negative actors emerge. As an industry, we can't truly represent a global society if we don't reflect the population we serve. I believe there's a desire for change, but the industry hasn't yet figured out how to implement and sustain that change consistently. It hasn't learned how to take a time-out to reflect on what's needed. It hasn't fully gained the insights to implement habits of change and generate impact.

Authenticity

I think the finance industry can often feel very fake; it doesn't always seem real. Where I've made the most impact is by not sugarcoating things but remaining forthright and authentic. In an industry that often tells you what you want to hear instead of what you need to hear, this approach is invaluable.

Sure, there are forthright people out there, but many aren't truly authentic. They're often motivated by some objective rather than putting individuals at the forefront of their decisions. In financial services, it's all about people and relationships. No matter how great your product is, if you don't have the right people on your bus, you'll never reach your destination.

Those who don't take advantage of all the programming Alvista Loop offers miss out on the opportunity to attract, grow, and retain top talent. If organizations don't genuinely want to help their individuals grow both personally and professionally, they can't expect the organization itself to thrive. My goals are to help the industry become more representative of the overall population, and to utilize my authentic approach to create a ripple effect of genuine, positive behavior that can impact the finance industry.

Repeated Success

This is your opportunity to not only make a change but keep it going.

Every organization wants a cycle of repeated success. But to get there, you have to understand that individual growth inspires organizational growth. You have to create a full-circle program that fosters continual growth. The Alvista Loop process makes this possible.

I always feel great pride for the people who go through the empowerment process and especially for those who really embrace it. They overcome their fears and become open and honest with themselves about what they want to achieve. It's incredible to witness their "light bulb moments" that empower them into action. That's what reassures me that this process truly works. More importantly, it shows others that it works, too, and that inspires them to take action. This empowerment can ripple outward, encouraging them to empower others as well.

My Hope For You

My real wish is that every early-career person entering the financial services industry aspires to be a top executive within the field. I hope every organization seeks to help every member learn from others, whether with one year of experience or forty. I hope that every woman who joins the industry sees herself thriving long-term rather than just sticking around until a personal milestone makes her feel she has to leave. I hope that every individual takes the time to gain insight into their authentic selves and is empowered to generate impact for future generations. Ultimately, I want to change the composition of the industry so that it truly reflects the society we live in.

And my hope for you? I hope that you will attract, grow, and retain diverse talent by helping others unlock their purpose, impact, and performance.

CONCLUSION

"The future depends on what you do today."

— Mahatma Gandhi

Even as you read these words, the finance industry is struggling to adapt and change in a way that will carry it forward successfully into the future. To survive and thrive in the years ahead, it needs exceptional talent — smart, engaged people with a wide variety of backgrounds and experiences to draw on. Yet even as you read this, those vital future contributors are looking at the finance industry and choosing not to pursue it as a career option or walking away from their current roles.

Having read this book, you know why: lack of representation. When you look at an industry and don't see anyone who looks like you, shares your background, or shares your experiences, it's hard to believe that the industry will be a welcoming, nurturing place. It's hard to see yourself at these organizations that don't demonstrate a desire to help them grow personally and professionally, something highly valued by Millennial and Gen Z talent.

Fortunately, things don't have to stay as they are... especially if you're willing to do more than just read these pages.

To Create Change, You Must Step Up

A finance industry that can attract, grow, and retain a fully representative cohort of talent — one that mirrors the diverse and unique audiences it serves — is an industry with the potential to achieve an extraordinarily profitable and life-enhancing future for everyone involved. Yet, it won't happen by accident.

While we tend to think of the finance industry as monolithic, the reality is that companies are made of people and built by people. The industry boils down to individuals and individual choices. Individual growth inspires organizational growth. So, you can choose to "go with the flow," or you can choose to pursue a path of empowerment and growth.

When you choose empowerment and growth, that means getting to know yourself, working on your mindset, taking intentional actions, and making those actions a self-reinforcing power in your life. From there, you have the strength and capacity to lift up others, expanding and nurturing the potential of those around you. There is very little you can't achieve or help others achieve.

From an organizational perspective, this looks like investing in the development of the talent under your care. It means seeing that talent as a whole person and valuing that talent equally for who they are, above and beyond their day-to-day production, so that you derail the stereotype of "this company only cares what I produce; they don't care about me." It means creating an environment where "two and out" is no longer the norm, and multigenerational coworkers can all see a way to work together on a long-term and even life-long basis.

Does that seem idealistic? Unrealistic? It's different from where we are now, to be sure. Yet, it is an option you can choose, and that your organization can choose, to unlock a brighter, better future.

We Can All Move Past the Status Quo

Choosing to empower yourself and the organizations around you is a chance for all of us to move beyond the status quo. We've seen what has been and what is... but what do we choose for the future?

And indeed, a choice must be made. My hope is that this book has given you the starting inspiration that you need to take the next step forward, along with an understanding of how the Alvista Loop Empowerment Process and customized executive coaching can support you. You're not alone, helpless, or required to stand by while the world continues to undervalue and underperform the people counting on it to do better. You can be the change you want to see in the world and be the force for empowerment you want in your life and the finance industry as a whole.

I can't wait to see what insights you've gained and the impact we can have on the future generation of finance leaders.

FINAL THOUGHT

My "final thought" was a technique I started using when working at BNP Paribas. It was a final slide in a presentation or a final point I made in a speech. It is not intended to be an actual conclusion. Instead, it's intended to be thought-provoking. It's meant for the audience to consider just a few more things that build on what was already said. With this in mind, below are my final thoughts. Although a lot is repetitive from what was discussed in the book, I felt it was important to put my personal lens on the top 10 lessons I've learned over more than half a century. It's how I use my life experiences from growing up on a cattle farm to navigating the finance industry as a foundation for how I live my life and how I coach my clients.

1. **It's better to fail than to succeed. It's how you learn, grow, and live.**

    "Failure is the stepping stone to success."

    —A Proverb

I am competitive, so the idea of failure has always been difficult. As I embraced many experiences and a lot of failures, I realized that it is in adversity that I gain strength, and in comfort, I build complacency. In my late 20s, I adopted the motto: "Life begins at the end of your comfort zone." Some might say that my motto led me to quit my first job at 29, get married at 33, have kids at 35 & 36, and pivot careers at 44. I would say my motto gave me the strength to tamp down my trepidation, to face my fear, and to embrace my experiences. It emboldened me to blaze my trail.

2. It's okay to speak up. It generates trust and empowers others.

"The greatest tragedy of mankind comes from the inability of people to have thoughtful disagreement to find out what's true."

—Ray Dalio

I dislike it when people say, "To be honest...." as if they were being dishonest at other times. Many people don't appreciate my desire to be candid and forthright. Many may not share my point of view. I haven't always timed my statements well, and the timing and delivery of my opinions is a learning opportunity. However, I can only be authentic when I speak up. My goal is to do so in a constructive way. I don't want to apologize for who I am or what I believe. I want to be open to other points of view. I want to cultivate relationships, be in situations, live in communities, and be part of a society where we have the liberty of speech and respect for differences of opinion.

3. **It's okay to have enemies. They allow you to cherish and cultivate relationships that matter.**

"I chose my friends for their good looks, my acquaintances for their good characters, and my enemies for their good intellects."

–Oscar Wilde

Relationships matter. They are vital to our mental and emotional well-being. Positive relationships can increase happiness and longevity. Negative relationships can lead to feelings of insecurity, depression, and even physical manifestations like heart problems. Over 50 years, I've learned to embrace positive relationships and appreciate negative associations. I learned to recognize certain professional enemies for the cutthroat people they are so that I can appreciate mentors who shaped my career. I've learned to acknowledge my poor choices in boyfriends for the liars and cheaters they were so I can cherish my husband. I've learned to identify people's motives to understand it is better to have an enemy who speaks against me to my face than to have a fake friend who speaks about me behind my back. I cherish my enemies, for they teach me to recognize true friends.

4. **It's okay to be silent. It allows you to hear what others have to say.**

"When you talk, you are only repeating what you already know. But if you listen, you may learn something new."

–Dalai Lama

Growing up, my grandfather often said, "Children should be seen and not heard." I always assumed he didn't think we had anything worthwhile to contribute to the conversation. Later, I learned that similar to the 9th-century Arabic proverb, "Speech is silver, silence is golden," my grandfather was encouraging me to learn more by praising the value of silence over speech.

This proverb has transcended time, crossing into song lyrics, memes, and movie catchphrases. It has become a philosophy used for parenting, social relationships, and professional situations. As Dr. Ralph Nichols stated, "The most basic of all human needs is the need to understand and be understood. The best way to understand people is to listen to them." Now, more than ever, in a world full of noise and rhetoric, a society focused on tweets, snaps, and DMs, it is important to listen to each other. The more I listen, the more I learn. The more I listen, the more I understand other points of view. The more I listen, the more I hear. I try to live as Epictetus, a Greek philosopher, once said, "We have two ears and one mouth so that we can listen twice as much as we speak."

5. **It's okay to discipline your kids (and yourself). It teaches them (and you) how to cope with disappointment.**

> *"The pain of discipline is nothing like the pain of disappointment."*
>
> —Justin Langer

Growing up, my dad used the "board of education" to teach me and my brothers right from wrong. I still remember the feeling of my dad's discipline. It was nothing compared to the disappointment in his eyes when I made poor choices. Many of those choices were made in the heat of the moment when I didn't stop to think things through. What I've learned is that if I use discipline, if I force myself to take a beat before reacting, I tend to make better choices and avoid disappointment.

6. **It's okay to change your mind. It shows you are surrounded by those who challenge you.**

"Surround yourself with people that push you to do better. No drama or negativity. Just higher goals and higher motivation. Good times and positive energy. No jealousy or hate. Simply bringing out the absolute best in each other."

—Warren Buffett

I love sitting and getting to know people and what makes them tick. I enjoy hearing their stories, understanding their perspectives, and considering how their backgrounds and experiences make them who they are. I believe that every person with whom I connect impacts who I am as a person. Part of growing as a person is valuing the people who are part of your life, for a short time or for a lifetime. Not everyone will be my BFF or a long-term professional colleague. Some are simply acquaintances. What I have found valuable in every aspect of my life, whether as a mom, a daughter, a colleague, a coach, or a friend, is that people shape who I am, but the right people make me a better person.

7. It's okay to be competitive. It teaches you what is worth the fight.

"Make your fighting stance your everyday stance."

−Musashi

The American dream is based on competing. Dominating in a sport is about competing. Excelling in school is about competing. Succeeding in your career is about competing. It's acceptable to be competitive regardless of what others might say, or what society deems 'too competitive.' Be competitive, but recognize that the greatest competition is against yourself. Outperforming others can be rewarding, but competing against yourself allows your own values and metrics to be the measure of your true happiness.

8. It's okay to be confident. It reinforces self-value and creates a role model.

"Self-confidence is more powerful than physical strength."

−Unknown

I've gained confidence over my life by putting myself in uncomfortable situations both personally and professionally. I learned to embrace imposter syndrome, to 'fake it until I made it,' and practiced power poses. I learned that my confidence grew more from my failures than my successes. I learned to embrace my insecurities (I have many) and to use my self-doubt to make me stronger. I accepted times in my life when I couldn't feel confident; it doesn't exist 100% of the time. I failed and made many mistakes, but each situation taught me that I could adapt, learn, and overcome. It illuminated what I could achieve and reinforced my self-value. It encouraged me to show my vulnerability alongside my confidence to be a role model to others.

9. **It's okay not to "have it all." It teaches you to prioritize and live life in harmony.**

"The secret to having it all is knowing you already do."
                                                                    –Unknown

---

One of my favorite quotes from Sheryl Sandberg is, "I have never met a woman, or man, who stated emphatically, 'Yes, I have it all.' Because no matter what any of us has—and how grateful we are for what we have—no one has it all." I completely agree. I don't believe we can have it all. What we can achieve is harmony in our lives, acknowledge what is important to us, and prioritize it above other things. For me, over the years, it was determining the balance of personal, professional, emotional, and physical pursuits and knowing what was important for me, not anyone else, that allowed me to find my happiness. So, I encourage everyone to recognize what is important for them, not what society deems important, and with that, you will achieve having YOUR all.

10. It's okay to be fired from a job. It teaches you resiliency and self-worth, and demonstrates intelligence that is lacking in the company's management.

"Getting fired is nature's way of telling you that you had the wrong job in the first place."

—Hal Lancaster

Getting fired altered my life. At first, I was angry that management failed to do their due diligence and that they took the easy road rather than making the "right choice." I quickly came to terms with the fact that those colleagues who I thought would have my back were only after self-preservation. I learned a life lesson about true friendship, authentic mentors, and competent leadership. Pivoting showed me that no matter where I am, no matter whether I'm working for myself or an organization, it is me that makes things succeed. It also confirmed what I have known all my life — I am resilient; I am valuable to myself and to others, and the lack of character in others reflects them, not me.

My final wish for you is that as you think about who you are, who you want to be, where your passion comes from, and who you want in your personal and professional life. Appreciate each experience that has shaped your thoughts, actions, and relationships. Use that knowledge to propel you forward to achieve your goals. Life is a long journey, and it begins outside your comfort zone.

ABOUT THE AUTHOR

Stephanie Hockman founded Alvista Loop to address a need in the financial services industry to attract, grow, and retain top diverse talent. Through her over 30 years working in or for the finance industry, she has gained experience that helps early career professionals, mid and senior level executives, women, and traditionally underrepresented individuals excel in their financial services career. She has a proven ability to coach individuals and collaborate with employers to enhance performance, improve productivity and drive long-term success.

Stephanie is a certified executive coach with over 23 years of experience in the finance industry and almost a decade of experience coaching and placing diverse, early career talent in the finance industry. Stephanie has experience coaching individuals and building teams and business lines in investment banks, private investing firms, alternative investment vehicles, startups, and higher education institutions.

Stephanie was the inaugural Program Director for the Careers in Business and Finance at Amherst College where she coaches, advises, and prepares students for careers in finance. In addition, she has collaborated with employers to develop recruiting processes that attract and retain diverse talent. Through her efforts, over one-third of the student population secures jobs in finance, consulting or general business.

Prior to Amherst College, Stephanie spent 23 years in the financial services industry. She worked at BNP Paribas as a Managing Director in Global Equities and Commodity Derivatives ("GECD") leading teams in New York, London, and Hong Kong. She was an inaugural member of the Women's Leadership Initiative, was a member of the GECD Executive Committee, founded the Women in Global Markets group, and led the GECD Summer Internship Program. Prior to BNP Paribas, Stephanie was a Principal at Banc of America Securities where she led the U.S. Prime Services client relationship management team. Through her tenure at Banc of America Securities, she increased client profitability and optimized resources to best align services and profitability and built a strong team culture of client service that received #1 ratings in industry surveys. She was also instrumental in transitioning almost 700 clients and over 300 employees from Bank of America to BNP Paribas at the height of the financial crisis. Stephanie started her career at Arthur Andersen providing tax consulting to hedge funds and investment partnerships and developed a growth strategy for the hedge fund advisory group. She was also the lead recruiter for the internship and full-time programs within the hedge fund practice. Throughout her career in the financial services industry, Stephanie has a proven track record of developing people, teams, and business lines, and has always been a leading figure for women in the organizations.

Stephanie received her Bachelor of Business Administration (BBA) and Master in Professional Accounting (MPA) at The University of Texas at Austin. She is a Board Certified Coach and received her coaches training from the Center for Executive Coaching. She also has her Hogan Assessments and MBTI certifications as well as several additional training certifications.

Stephanie enjoys spending time with her husband and two children.